Aspiring to be Global

T0293028

ENCOUNTERS

Series Editors: Jan Blommaert, *Tilburg University, The Netherlands*, Ben Rampton, *Kings College London, UK*, Anna De Fina, *Georgetown University, USA*, Sirpa Leppänen, *University of Jyväskylä, Finland* and James Collins, *University at Albany/SUNY, USA*

The Encounters series sets out to explore diversity in language from a theoretical and an applied perspective. So the focus is both on the linguistic encounters, inequalities and struggles that characterise post-modern societies and on the development, within sociocultural linguistics, of theoretical instruments to explain them. The series welcomes work dealing with such topics as heterogeneity, mixing, creolization, bricolage, cross-over phenomena, polylingual and polycultural practices. Another high-priority area of study is the investigation of processes through which linguistic resources are negotiated, appropriated and controlled, and the mechanisms leading to the creation and maintenance of sociocultural differences. The series welcomes ethnographically oriented work in which contexts of communication are investigated rather than assumed, as well as research that shows a clear commitment to close analysis of local meaning making processes and the semiotic organisation of texts.

All books in this series are externally peer-reviewed.

Full details of all the books in this series and of all our other publications can be found on http://www.multilingual-matters.com, or by writing to Multilingual Matters, St Nicholas House, 31-34 High Street, Bristol BS1 2AW, UK.

ENCOUNTERS: 13

Aspiring to be Global

Language and Social Change in a Tourism Village in China

Shuang Gao

MULTILINGUAL MATTERS
Bristol • Blue Ridge Summit

DOI https://doi.org/10.21832/GAO2753
Library of Congress Cataloging in Publication Data
A catalog record for this book is available from the Library of Congress.

Names: Gao, Shuang, author.
Title: Aspiring to be Global: Language and Social Change in a Tourism Village in
    China/Shuang Gao.
Description: Bristol, UK, Blue Ridge Summit, PA: Multilingual Matters, 2019. |
    Series: Encounters: 13 | Includes bibliographical references and index.
Identifiers: LCCN 2018046305| ISBN 9781788922753 (hbk : alk. paper) |
    ISBN 9781788922777 (epub) | ISBN 9781788922784 (kindle)
Subjects: LCSH: Languages in contact—China—Yangshuo Xian. |
    Sociolinguistics—China—Yangshuo Xian. | Chinese language—Globalization. |
    English language—China—Yangshuo Xian. | English language—Influence on
    Chinese.
Classification: LCC P40.5.L382 C557 2019 | DDC 306.4409512/8—dc23 LC record
    available at https://lccn.loc.gov/2018046305

British Library Cataloguing in Publication Data
A catalogue entry for this book is available from the British Library.

ISBN-13: 978-1-78892-275-3 (hbk)
ISBN-13: 978-1-78892-099-5 (pbk)

Multilingual Matters
UK: St Nicholas House, 31-34 High Street, Bristol BS1 2AW, UK.
USA: NBN, Blue Ridge Summit, PA, USA.

Website: www.multilingual-matters.com
Twitter: Multi_Ling_Mat
Facebook: https://www.facebook.com/multilingualmatters
Blog: www.channelviewpublications.wordpress.com

The policy of Multilingual Matters/Channel View Publications is to use papers
that are natural, renewable and recyclable products, made from wood grown in
sustainable forests. In the manufacturing process of our books, and to further
support our policy, preference is given to printers that have FSC and PEFC Chain
of Custody certification. The FSC and/or PEFC logos will appear on those books
where full certification has been granted to the printer concerned.

Typeset by Deanta Global Publishing Services Limited.

Contents

Acknowledgments

First, I would like to thank the people I met during my fieldwork in Yangshuo. The story told here is theirs. This book would not have been possible had they not so kindly shared their stories with me in most helpful ways. They have made this research an enjoyable process. I learned so much from them, and was often overwhelmed by their hospitality. I can only hope the readers will appreciate their stories, if not the way I have told them.

I also want to thank many people for their scholarly support. I am most grateful to Joseph Sung-Yul Park and Ben Rampton. I could not have undertaken this research project without the encouragement of Joseph. It is through many discussions with him that the research project took shape and finally got started. Ben dedicated so much time and effort to guide me through the research process, and was always ready to provide his insights on many issues. Needless to say, I am indebted to them for their patience, guidance and kind encouragement. I also received valuable feedback on various occasions from Lionel Wee, Constant Leung, Roxy Harris, Adrienne Lo, Kira Hall, John Gray, Miguel Pérez-Milans, Allan Bell, Monica Heller and Adam Jaworski. Their comments and feedback helped improve my work.

Chapters 3 and 5 were published previously in slightly altered forms as 'Commodification of place, consumption of identity: The sociolinguistic construction of a 'global village' in rural China' in the *Journal of Sociolinguistics* 16 (3), 336–357 in 2012, and 'Interactional straining and the neoliberal self: Learning English in the biggest English corner in China' in *Language in Society* 45 (3), 397–421 in 2016. I gratefully acknowledge permission from John Wiley and Sons and Cambridge University Press.

I also thank my book editor Jan Blommaert, whose work has always been a true inspiration, and the anonymous reviewer for very helpful and constructive comments. I also appreciate the kind help and professional support from everyone at the editorial team, especially Sarah Williams, Elinor Robertson, Flo McClelland, Jayanthi Chander and Anna Roderick.

Finally, my deepest thanks and love to my parents, for always believing in me and giving me the freedom to do what I like, and to my husband and family-in-law, for their unfailing care and support.

1 Introduction

Starting the Journey

This research originates from two main inspirational sources, one in the chair, another on the road. Back in May 2006, when I was about to finish my bachelor's at a university in Hunan Province, China, a couple of classmates suggested that we went on a graduation tour. We finally decided to go to Yangshuo County and the city of Guilin, which is located in the neighboring Guangxi Zhuang Autonomous Region (see Map 1.1) and is well known for its beautiful natural sceneries. As the popular saying goes: 'Guilin has the best scenery of mountains and rivers; Yangshuo boasts even better'. So, there we were on the road.

On the train, we found ourselves in the same carriage with another group of students. Actually, it was such a large group that we looked like outsiders; it quickly became apparent to us that it was 'their' carriage. With us were a cohort of college students, about a hundred of them, going to Yangshuo together with their teachers. I was told that they went there to practice English with foreigners. I had heard that Yangshuo was quite popular among foreign travelers, but the idea still intrigued me because I was not sure how they were going to do that. Maybe as intern tour guides, I supposed, but I quickly forgot about it as travel fatigue got to me.

After travelling around the city for about three days, we headed without out a break for Yangshuo. It takes some time to reach Yangshuo County from the city; however, unlike many journeys, the time on the road was not dull. As the bus left the city of Guilin behind, the views along the road were refreshing and soothing – rivers, Karst mountains, extensive farm lands. One would have a more intimate experience of the natural beauty if one chose to take a boat down the famous Li River that runs across the county from the city (see Figure 1.1). Indeed, Yangshuo has always been attractive. It is unique and well known among backpackers for its Karst

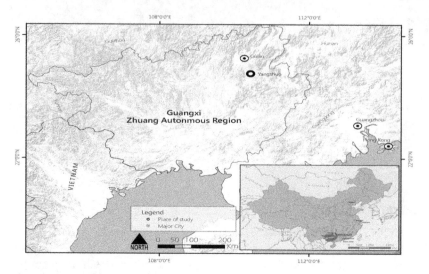

Map 1.1 Geographical location of Yangshuo (*Source*: Courtesy of Leonardo Zurita-Arthos)

geography; it was a resort for imperial officials during the Song Dynasty (1100s).

On arrival, we quickly found a nice and affordable hotel (a triple room for only 40 yuan per night) near Yangshuo bus station. Then, we were ready to exhaust the place and ourselves – cycling, mountain climbing,

Figure 1.1 Yangshuo scenery (*Source*: Photo by author, 2011)

bamboo rafting and other activities. That evening, one of my friends suggested that we went for a walk in a local street, West Street (西街 Xī Jiē). A traditional neighborhood street on the west bank, West Street winds into the town from the dock of the Li River. Over the last three decades, this street has been the place where many travelers take a short break after their journey or base themselves if they plan to further explore the countryside. It is not a very long street, several hundred meters, paved with large uneven black marble stones and lined by Ming-Qing-style residential buildings (see Figure 1.2). But further into the street, it is a different world. In contrast to the laid-back countryside, West Street is busy. At night, the street is lit up with colorful neon lights. Before you realize it, you are part of the crowd, passing souvenir shops and artistic craft tables, and seeing people of different color chatting over beer, coffee and pizza. I remember watching a foreigner with a white beard happily playing his guitar in front of a bar, smiling for the many tourists and their cameras. Obviously, he was much more at home than I was. After walking for a while, my friends insisted that we went for a drink in a bar. Amid colorful lights and live band music, a sense of displacement and uneasiness came over me, making me wonder how everything had ended up here in this small town in a faraway countryside. Never quite used to this kind of bustling nightlife, I quickly finished the worst lemon tea ever and left my friends to enjoy themselves. The next evening, as we used our cameras

Figure 1.2 West Street, Yangshuo (*Source*: Photo by author, 2011)

to capture one last picture of the sunset over the river while running to catch the last bus, I told myself I must come back again. I never expected, however, that I would return as a researcher.

This research is about West Street, Yangshuo, a changing place in a rapidly changing China. What brings me back to Yangshuo is a concern for the changing roles of language in its sociohistorical transformation. In the current phase of globalization, it has been observed that socioeconomic restructuring has led to the reconceptualization and re-evaluation of language, especially among ethnolinguistic communities. Notably, Heller's (2003) pioneering research 'Globalization, the new economy, and the commodification of language and identity' examines a tourism site in francophone Canada. She reveals how economic restructuring and entry into the global market has led to the re-evaluation of multilingual repertoires in francophone Canada and the valorization of the local variety of French for heritage tourism, which she succinctly describes as the entrance into the 'language industry' (Heller, 2010: 352; 2017). This strategy is also seen among other ethnolinguistic communities. Coupland et al. (2005) discuss the commodification of Welsh for the heritage tourism of mining in Wales. Thurlow and Jaworski (2010) show the use of minority languages in traveler's language textbooks and television tourism programs, which helps produce a sense of exoticness (see also Chen, 2016; Kelly-Holmes & Pietikainen, 2014; Sharma & Phyak, 2017; Wang, 2015).

The case of West Street, however, differs from the above-mentioned cases in that its sociohistorical transformation involves the mobilization and re-evaluation of non-local, instead of local, resources. While located in a region with multiple ethnolinguistic minorities, most notably Zhuang, the tourism development of Yangshuo in recent years has been capitalizing on the English language, as well as other semiotic resources, as opposed to local ethnolinguistic varieties. The image of foreigners living happily in Yangshuo figures prominently in the media, particularly in tourism promotional discourses targeting domestic Chinese tourists. West Street is advertised as a 'global village' (地球村) and an 'English Corner' (英语角) wherein Western elements, the English language in particular, are highlighted and indigenous local elements are downplayed if not erased.

This study thus seeks to examine the tourism site of West Street, Yangshuo, as an important case for the sociolinguistics of mobility. Blommaert (2010), in his seminal book *The Sociolinguistics of Globalization*, observes that there have been shifting perspectives in language and society, one of which involves a shift from a view in which language is narrowly tied to a community, a time and a place, and in which language is primarily seen as having local functions, to a view in which language exists in and for mobility across space and time. This shift, I would say, is conceptually far more momentous…, because it forces us to consider linguistic signs detached from their traditional locus of origin (in a speech community, and with a specific set of local functions), and instead replaced, so to speak, in a very different loci of production and uptake – where the conventional associative functions of such signs cannot be taken for granted… it is only when we think of linguistic signs as being very much 'open' signs, onto which several functions (simultaneously) can be projected, that we can start to find answers to the complex and often bewildering phenomenology of language in globalization. (Blommaert, 2010: 181–182)

Adopting this perspective, my research examines language as 'open signs' where the social meanings of language cannot be assumed or taken for granted, but can only be revealed by exploring the historical processes of meaning projection. More specifically, I investigate

- How has West Street become a so-called 'global village' and 'English Corner'?
- What roles do language and communication play in this process of social change?
- What are the implications of this sociohistorical change for the local community?

Through asking these questions, this research seeks to understand West Street's social change from the perspective of changing language ideologies and practices. As I will show below, the recent transformation of West Street, Yangshuo, into a 'global village' occurs in tandem with ideological and economic changes in China during the past few decades. In this sense, it represents a 'telling case' (Heath & Street, 2008: 64) of the complexities, contingencies and tensions involved in China's globalization process.

Before providing a proper introduction to Yangshuo, however, it would be useful to explain first what tourism is, and how I approach the tourism site in question. I will suggest that tourism provides one important domain for understanding the sociolinguistics of mobility, both theoretically and empirically. I then introduce the tourism site of West Street, Yangshuo, focusing on several aspects of its recent social change from a global, national and local nexus. I then provide a theoretical framework for the present study, discussing the key concepts of globalization, mobility, locality and historicity. An overview of the book is provided at the end of the chapter.

Tourism as a Social Field

Tourism is often considered the biggest industry in the world and represents 'the largest movement of human populations outside wartime' (Crick, 1989: 310, as cited in Wang, 2000: 1; see also Dann, 1996). It has been a topic of research in disciplines as varied as geography, economics, anthropology, sociology and sociolinguistics (see e.g. Dann, 1996; Nash & Smith, 1991; Stronza, 2001; Thurlow & Jaworski, 2010). This multidisciplinary exploration of tourism, however, does not mean that tourism has always been a key concern in social sciences (Wang, 2000: 1). Indeed, tourism itself cannot yet claim to have its own disciplinary integrity and has been having difficulty finding itself a disciplinary home (Dann & Cohen, 1991; Leite & Graburn, 2009). It is therefore not surprising that definitions of tourism vary not only across disciplines, but also according to the specific theoretical perspectives one takes within one discipline (Dann & Cohen, 1991; Leite & Graburn, 2009; Nash, 1981; Wang, 2000).

This is not necessarily something regretful. Indeed, Dean MacCannell, one of the founding scholars of tourism, suggests that the significance of tourism research lies in exposing 'a deep flaw in discipline thought':

> Whatever its methodological or theoretical orientation, and even when it does not intend to do so, tourism research exposes a deep flaw in discipline thought: specifically, a methodological commitment to, or at least a dependence upon, the assumption of cultural homogeneity within the various fields of study ... But mainly (and this is their central failing when it comes to analysis of current social forms), sociology, anthropology, psychology, economics, political science, even history, operates *as if* their subject matter is framed by a single culture, unifying logic, intersubjective agreement, parallel intentions, and motivations. (MacCannell, 1989: 2, italics original)

One telling example might be the conception of tourists. The study of the 'tourist' originated from an embarrassing situation when 'in the 1960s, some anthropologists were struck by the intrusion of tourists into their field' (Leite & Graburn, 2009: 39). As mentioned earlier, due to the disciplinary bias of documenting the 'authentic', many anthropologists adopted an attitude of resistance by either ignoring tourists during fieldwork, in particular when they themselves could be (mis)taken for tourists, or intentionally omitting tourists from their publications (Leite & Graburn, 2009: 38–39; see also Graburn, 2002). This is especially the case when tourists could also claim knowledge about the field. Such disciplinary practice based on assumptions of homogeneity or rigorous commitment to the uncontaminated, isolated and therefore authentic, MacCannell (1989: 2–3; c.f. Pratt, 1987) argues, has resulted in the exclusion of those social forms that are 'emerging, new, unplanned, unstable; shaping thought and behavior in still unknown ways'. In this sense, it is a groundbreaking epistemological statement when Nash (1981: 461) states that 'at the heart of any definition of tourism is the person we conceive to be a tourist'. Over the past decade, scholars in tourism research have been debating over how to move toward a post-disciplinary perspective and rethink tourism not just theoretically but ontologically (see e.g. Winter, 2009: 22–23). Recently, this need for rethinking has been most strongly advocated by Sheller and Urry (2006) who propose a 'new mobilities paradigm':

> Social science has largely ignored or trivialized the importance of the systemic movements of people for work and family life, for leisure and pleasure, and for politics and protest. The paradigm challenges the ways in which much social science research has been 'a-mobile'. … Travel has been for the social sciences seen as a black box, a neutral set of technologies and processes predominantly permitting forms of economic, social, and political life that are seen as explicable in terms of other, more causally powerful processes. (Sheller & Urry, 2006: 208)

On a more general level, they observe that:

> Social science has thus been static in its theory and research. It has not sufficiently examined how, enhanced by various objects and technologies, people move. But also it has not seen how images and communications are also intermittently on the move and those actual and potential movements organize and structure social life. (Sheller & Urry, 2006: 212)

It is in this mobility turn that tourism research gets most integrated with social science (see Cohen & Cohen, 2012; Leite & Graburn, 2009: 52; Mavrič & Urry, 2009). Taking this mobility perspective, my analytical scope is not confined to touristic activities in a narrow sense (c.f. Cohen, 1984)[1]; rather, I explore the tourism site of West Street, Yangshuo, as what Leite and Graburn (2009) term 'a social field':

an anthropological approach precludes viewing tourism as a distinct entity in itself, to be defined everywhere in the same way. It is, instead, 'not one, but many sets of practices, with few clear boundaries but some central ideas' (Abram et al. 1997: 2), all embedded within broader social, political, and historical framework. As a cultural phenomenon, its significant components will shift depending on one's starting point. Thus 'tourism' can refer to a category of experience counterposed to everyday life; a local, national, or global industry; an opportunity for employment; a source of strangers in one's home locality; a force for social change; a form of cultural representation and brokerage; an emblem and a medium of globalization; a venue for the construction and performance of national, ethnic, gendered, and other identities; or any combination of these and more. Tourism is thus most productively viewed not as an entity in its own right, but instead as a social field in which many actors engage in complex interactions across time and space, both physical and virtual … [so as] to explore the ambiguities, contingencies, and slippages revealed in the particularities of each instance. The resulting body of scholarship attends to how actual people understand and conduct their involvement in the interrelated practices of travelling, encountering, guiding, producing, representing, talking, moving, hosting, and consuming. (Leite & Graburn, 2009: 37)

This approach enables us to explore the embeddedness of tourism sites and touristic activities within larger social structures across time and space, as well as the contingencies and tensions involved. For our purpose here, it also has implications for the politics of knowledge production. With the rise of Asian tourists during the past decade (Cohen & Cohen 2012; Winter, 2009) and China's likely domination of the global tourism market in 2020, as predicted by the World Tourism Organization (Nyíri, 2009: 153), it is important to ask whether Asian tourism can be explained by existing tourism research established from an ethnocentric perspective. As Winter (2009) notes:

Given that the paradigm of tourism has in large part been constructed around an analysis of west-to-east, north-to-south encounters, rooted in ideas of globalization as a process of westernization, our tourist has been silently conceived as white (and male). (Winter, 2009: 23–24; see also Cohen & Cohen, 2012: 2195)

Indeed, after the Second World War, postcolonial countries were first advised by their former colonizers to establish tourism sites to regain economic development (Leite & Graburn, 2009: 40). This neocolonial practice helps perpetuate the presumption that Asia is on the receiving end of tourism mobilities. Approaching tourism as a social field helps avoid such ethnocentrism and theoretical reductionism, and enables us to appreciate the empirical richness and complexities of tourism in Asia. A first step, as Winter (2009: 28) suggests, is to make up for 'the lack of historical accounts' on Asian tourism by 'situat[ing] the historical growth of travel ... within their appropriate societal changes'. This is the task of the next section.

Yangshuo: A Brief Introduction

Yangshuo County (1436.91 km²) is located in the southeast of Guilin City, Guangxi Zhuang Autonomous Region in southern China. The region, as its name indicates, has the largest number of Zhuang ethnic people, accounting for more than 90% of the Zhuang population in China. In Yangshuo County, according to the 2003 statistics, 12.6% (37,760) of the residents (299,434) are from minority groups including Zhuang, Yao, Hui, Miao, Tibetan, Dong and others, though the majority of the population is Han. Historical study indicates that Yangshuo as a county was established as early as the year 590, though the earliest written record of the county, as available now, could only be traced to the Qing Dynasty (1673). 'West Street' got its name in the year 1674 for no other reason than it is on the west bank of the Li River (Wang, 2006a: 112–113). Below, I briefly introduce the recent transformation of Yangshuo, contextualizing the process against wider economic, cultural and social changes. Specifically, I focus on the changing ideologies of mobility, the depoliticization of tourism and the management of linguistic and cultural diversity.

Changing ideologies of mobility

For most of their recent history, Yangshuo people have been living a simple life of agriculture and fishery, but they have always been closely connected with the outside world. While located in a relatively remote region, Yangshuo's geographic location near the Li River has made it a favorable transit spot for businesspersons when freight transportation was mainly dependent on boats and ships. Also, in the early half of the 20th century, a period of social turmoil caused by international and domestic wars, people from the neighboring provinces of Jiangxi, Guangdong and Hunan also arrived because of war and famine (Wang, 2006a: 117–118). Around this time, several guilds were established for people from the same hometown. At Guangdong Guild, an English language editor from a Shanghai publishing house came for shelter and was invited to run the first English workshop. In the 1940s, a foreign language training center for Kuomintang (the Chinese Nationalist Party) officials also moved to Yangshuo to train embassy interpreters and translators; there were foreign expatriates as well. Apart from one or two Western preachers (Wang, 2006: 121), the establishment of a prisoner-of-war camp in Yangshuo during the anti-Japanese War and the Second World War also brought in large numbers of foreign people, mainly Germans, Japanese and Italians, as the Nationalist Party of China moved to Yangshuo. This period thus witnessed a sudden and temporary growth in the population from only 2,500 to around 10,000 people (Wang, 2006a: 122).

A relatively stable, though short-lived, time came with the establishment of the People's Republic of China in 1949. Instead of being passively caught up in the various mobilities of people and goods, attempts were made by the local and national governments to develop the area as a tourism spot in consideration of its natural beauty. However, these development initiatives failed to be implemented because of the Cultural Revolution (1966–1976). Under the Mao regime, the geographical mobilities of Chinese people were sanctioned mainly by two governance systems, *hukou* and *danwei*. The former is residential registration, used to position Chinese citizens in their birthplaces through spatial differentiation of social welfare. This includes rural–urban as well as intercity differentiation (for details, see Cheng & Selden, 1994). The latter danwei, also known as work unit, involved the monitoring and management of working staff. The work unit functioned as an immediate authority for each employee in almost every aspect of their working and private life, including marriage, childbirth and much more (see Hoffman, 2010). There was mass population movement from the 1950s to the 1970s, but this was mainly the movement of millions of urban intellectuals to rural farmlands to be re-educated, especially during the Cultural Revolution (1966–1976). During this time, even the street name 'West Street', containing the word 'west', suddenly became politically incorrect and had to be changed to 'East Wind Street', until 1982 when those cultural sanctions were finally eradicated (Wang, 2006a: 113–114). Around the same time, with the collapse of the Sino–Russia relationship, the Russian language was replaced with the English language in China's foreign language policy, though only basic English was taught in order to advocate Maoist doctrines during the Cultural Revolution (see Ji, 2004; Wang, 2006a). Therefore, until the Open-up and Reform in 1978, West Street had mostly been a typical traditional street where people lived in traditional houses and occasionally sold extra agriculture products just in front of their own homes.

The year 1978 is widely recognized as the starting point for the globalization process in modern China. The year marked the coming to power of Deng Xiaoping, whose wisdom was to set China on a fast-paced economic development, albeit fraught with increasing inequalities, through his reform and open-up policy (see Harvey, 2005: Chapter 5). The implementation of this policy is often considered China's second revolution, after the establishment of the People's Republic of China (Xiao, 2006: 803), and it is still an important government policy today. This policy marked the end of the centralized planned economy, and the start of economic reform toward a market economy with Chinese characteristics. The early reforms were gradual but still generated problems that finally led to the Tiananmen Square protests in 1989. This political event created much uncertainty within the Communist Party, and there were divergent opinions within the party as to how exactly to continue with the reform policy (Zheng, 2014). Nevertheless, Deng's south China tour in 1992 was significant in showing the party's resolution on China's reform. After this year, more decisive policies and measures started to be implemented, which set China in motion, in particular through internal labor migration (Bian, 2009).

Mobilities for Chinese people no longer just means the freedom to move geographically, it also means breaking through the spatial constraints attached to their daily and working lives under the previous bureaucratic system, moving out of their designated spatial order and relocating to a place of their own choice while adjusting themselves to the social organizations of the new space they are in.[2] Mobility, at this important turning point in a changing China, therefore marks the beginning of new ways of living for Chinese people.

The above account shows that China is set in motion through its reform and open policy, most evidently after Deng's south China tour in 1992. But if we broaden our scope and position China within the world context, we see that while large-scale mobilities *within* the modern Chinese society only started in the early 1990s, mobilities *into* China happened much earlier, in particular through the tourism industry. Tourism has played, and is still playing, an important role politically, economically and culturally, in China's globalization process, as we will see below.

Depoliticizing tourism and entering the global order

As noted by Urry (2002: 142–143), 'in certain cases becoming a tourist destination is part of a reflexive process by which societies and places come to enter the global order'. This is exactly the case in China, and in Yangshuo in particular. The development of the tourism industry was an important part of Deng's open and reform policy. As Xiao (2006) shows, in a matter of 10 months from October 1978 to July 1979, Deng gave five directional talks on China's tourism development as an important part of his open and reform policy, in order to improve international relations and achieve economic development. This was a sharp departure from the Mao era, when 'travel to the PRC was forbidden by the United States and many other western governments. China reciprocated by generally denying entry to most foreigners' (Ritcher, 1989: 24, as cited in Xiao, 2006: 804). This sudden opening of the door was recorded by early international tourists as follows:

> After being closed for repairs for almost 30 years the Middle Kingdom suddenly swung open its big red doors – but not quite all the way. Comrades! We must increase the production of tourists! China desperately needs the foreign exchange that tourism so conveniently provides, and it has done very well out of the deal so far. With several million tourists flocking in every year, the tallest buildings in China are, appropriately, hotels. Come back in five years' time and there'll be Marco Polo Pizza Bars dotting the Great Wall.
>
> In the late 1970s the tour groups started rolling in but the prospects for individual travel looked extremely dim. It has always been possible for individuals to travel to the PRC, but by invitation only, and until the late 1970s few managed an invite. The first regulars were people from Sweden and France (nations favored by China) who stepped off the Trans-Siberian in 1979 when it reopened after 30 years.
>
> In 1981 the Chinese suddenly started issuing visas to solo and uninvited travelers through a couple of their embassies overseas, but mainly through various agencies in Hong Kong. Just about anyone who wanted a visa could get one, but since there was no fanfare, news spread slowly by word of mouth. By 1983 it seemed that just about everyone who landed in Hong Kong was going to China. After all, we'd been waiting over 30 years to travel in the country unfettered by tour guides. (*Lonely Planet China*, 1988: 7)

In contrast to the favorable policy toward international tourism, however, the prospect of a domestic tourism market was slim. As Nyíri (2009: 153) notes, 'before 1978, …tourism, which in any case lacked any significant domestic tradition, …was regarded as part of the bourgeois lifestyle and, as such, taboo'. But even 'as late as the mid-1990s, the issue of whether China should support or discourage domestic tourism was contentious within government circles. Its opponents argued that tourism bred immoral behavior, wasted resources and distracted the population from productive activities' (Nyíri, 2009: 153–154).

The establishment of the domestic tourism market finally took shape in the year 1998, albeit through what Nyíri (2009: 153) calls a 'precipitous decision'. This is because such endorsement came at a time after the Asian financial crisis when the government 'faced an urgent need to increase domestic consumer demand' (Nyíri, 2009: 153; see also Zhang, 2003). Nevertheless, such initiatives were compatible with an already changing China wherein internal migration and labor mobility were becoming a new way of living. In other words, tourism became another form of mobility for Chinese people, which not only helped form a leisure market but was also a means of searching for new lifestyles and identity in a consumer society (Nyíri, 2009: 153; see also Arlt, 2008).

The promotion of domestic consumption also represents an important transformation in China's economic development strategy. In the late 1990s, a series of events made China realize that the interconnectivity of the world would position China in an unfavorably constrained condition if it continued its export-oriented and production-based economy. Domestic consumption was thus explicitly stated as the 'new source', 'new impetus', 'main engine' for China's long-term economic growth (Croll, 2006: 1). This turn toward a consumer society is also reflected in the new vocabularies used to describe certain lifestyles, such as *bobos*, a mixed style of bourgeois and bohemian; *neo-neo-tribe*, a teenage style of exaggeration and uniqueness; *non-mainstream*, a less expensive but equally fashionable style. As Wang (2005) shows, these labels have been used as a marketing strategy in commercial advertisings that satisfy the Chinese consumer psychology of what Veblen calls 'pecuniary emulation', that is, a tiered logic of consumption wherein emulating a higher lifestyle is considered the fastest way of acquiring social prestige (Wang, 2005: 532). Against this context, tourism, which had been denigrated as a bourgeois and capitalist activity, started to be a celebrated consumer activity in this national turn toward a consumer society.

Of particular interest to the present study is the term 'xiǎozī' (小资), which refers to people aspiring to Western lifestyles and valuing worldliness, fashion and hedonism, including the use of foreign languages (Bao, 2002). In short, it is about taste and style, particularly among young urban dwellers who have not yet achieved middle-class economic status (c.f. Wang, 2005).[3] As I will show below, the 'global village' of West Street, Yangshuo, represents to a large extent what globalization means to lower-middle-class Chinese people. Chapter 3, in particular, shows how the 'global village' packages various semiotic resources for xiǎozī lifestyles.

Apart from this particularity of domestic tourism in China, another point worth mentioning is how the development of the tourism industry in China is also characterized by a rural–urban differentiation. As Xiao (2006: 811) observes, 'unlike Mao's victory in establishing the People's Republic, which started from the rural to besiege the urban, the story of China's tourism unfolded in the opposite way – starting from urban areas and dominated by sightseeing and mass tourism. Inevitably, planning for tourism also involves urban design and (re)construction'.

The county of Yangshuo was already officially designated as one of the first places in China open to international travelers in 1978, but its significance was largely recognized due to its geographical closeness to the city of Guilin, which is also famous for its beautiful sceneries (Jiang, 2009: 198). The importance of the Li River as a scenic attraction, which runs across the city and the county, was highlighted by Deng Xiaoping during his two trips to the city of Guilin in 1978 and 1986 (Xiao, 2006: 809–810). Additionally, the Guangxi government had dedicated much effort to the development of the city of Guilin, and different proposals were made to establish it as a 'modern industrial city' (1959); 'Eastern Geneva: a scenery city with Chinese characteristics' (1963); 'socialist city with beautiful sceneries, modern industry, modern agriculture, modern science and culture' (1973) (*Contemporary China: Guangxi*, 2009: 359). Such development policies meant that Yangshuo had to passively depend on the city of Guilin in terms of its tourist sources – becoming a tourist destination for Yangshuo was more of a political mission assigned by the central government to earn badly needed foreign currencies for the young China (Su & Teo, 2009; Zhang, 2003) instead of a local economic development priority. Therefore, unsurprisingly, in the early 1980s, Yangshuo barely managed to prepare itself for these early tourists, as recorded by the early Lonely Planet tourist-writers:

> In 1983, when the first edition of this book was being researched, there wasn't much in Yangshuo. The tourist market by the dock catered to the flotilla of tour boats bearing Chinese, Japanese and westerners who swept through like a plague of locusts before being bundled on buses and whisked back to Guilin. Three hotels (one of which they wouldn't let you stay at, and another which didn't have toilets) and a couple of soupy noodle dispensaries catered to the meager number of backpackers who found their way here. (*Lonely Planet China*, 1988: 607)

The situation lasted until the 1990s when initiatives were finally taken by the local Yangshuo government to support tourism as an important industry. With the depoliticization of tourism as an industry and with further privatization of business operations under the market economy, the local government in 1985 started to recognize tourism as one part of the local economy, though agriculture and fisheries still accounted for much of the local revenue. But since the 1990s, against the background of China's more aggressive turn toward a market economy, the significance of tourism as an industry has been recognized and even prioritized by the local Yangshuo government. The importance of Yangshuo as a tourism site was also highlighted by two national government officials – the then Prime Minister Li Peng and former President Yang Shangkun. In their separate visits to Yangshuo in 1996, both declared in calligraphy writing the importance of Yangshuo as a tourism site: 'Yangshuo, A Famous Tourism County in China' by Li Peng and 'Yangshuo, the No. 1 Tourism County in China' by Yang Shangkun (*A Fast-Developing Tourism County*, 1999: 3). The various aspects and specifics of this historical change toward a tourism economy in Yangshuo will be explained in the following empirical chapters.

During this time, local residents started to engage in tourism businesses to improve their own living conditions and, as it turned out, their 'small businesses... complemented the entire tourism supply system that state-owned tourism enterprises could not fully cover' (Gao *et al.*, 2009: 441). Some local people then started to set up small family businesses catering to international travelers. But they only learned to use English or Japanese as they communicated with foreign travelers, and it was not rare to see people communicating through body language. Some chose to sell 'antiques'. 'Most people, at the beginning', as one local business owner told me, 'they just searched for old wooden boards or "ancient" stones, and sold them. That's it. Those kinds of old stuff, which looked like ancient treasures. Hahaha. They were just not sure about what they should sell to the foreigners'. Others were more entrepreneurial and experimented with opening their own businesses at this early stage of China's market economy, learning to make and sell Western food. In 1988, 'you can munch on banana pancakes and muesli, slurp coffee and hang out in half a dozen or more travelers' cafés with Midnight Oil and Dire Straits tapes playing in the background' (*Lonely Planet China*, 1988: 607).

Since then, this small, laid-back neighborhood has gained increasing popularity among international travelers:

Just 1.5 hours from Guilin by bus, Yangshuo has ...become one of those legendary backpacker destinations that most travelers have heard about long before they even set foot in China. ... Yangshuo is still a great laid-back base from which to explore other small villages in the nearby countryside. With its western-style cafes, Hollywood movies, Bob Marley tunes and banana pancakes, Yangshuo may not seem like the 'real China', but who cares? It's a great spot to relax, see the scenery and grab a good cup of coffee-the perfect antidote to weeks or months on the road. Don't make this your first or second stop coming from Hong Kong. Save it for after knocking around Guangzhou or Guangxi for a spell. You'll appreciate it much more. (*Lonely Planet China*, 1998: 774)

From the late 1990s, the national media reports started to portray West Street as a 'global village'. As I will show below, it would be a simplification to conclude that the 'global village' is a result of the inflow of international tourists, though that does contribute to the observed social change. The popularity of the site among domestic tourists indicates other national factors at work, in particular what the 'global village' means to Chinese people.

Managing diversity

Tourism mobilities, both domestic and foreign, contribute to the cultural and linguistic diversity of tourism sites. It is important, therefore, to note how in an already multi-ethnic China, multiple diversities are perceived by the public and managed by the state. Below, I briefly explain two aspects of diversity: ethnic diversity, which points to the peculiarity and difficulty of minority language valorization in China; and foreign migrants to China, which is related to the emergence of a unique language learning event, the English Corner.

Farrer (2014: 19) notes that, 'multiculturalism in China has been conceptualized primarily in terms of relations between the majority Han population and the ethnic minorities'. He further elaborates that:

China's current politics of multiculturalism was developed in a twentieth-century context of colonialism, invasion, and national resistance. Upon seizing power in 1949, the Communist Party rapidly moved to assert control of minority border regions that had in some cases gained *de facto* independence or were occupied by foreign powers. In contrast to the previous regime of the Republic of China that downplayed the very existence of ethnic minorities in China, the CCP [Chinese Communist Party] employed the rhetoric of a multi-ethnic nation and political self-determination to stave off independence movements and counter the involvement of foreign powers in border regions. ... Despite the rhetoric of cultural diversity and political autonomy, the Party's desire to assert control over these resource rich and strategically important border regions meant that China's multicultural policies have always involved an unstated goal of assimilating 'backward' minority populations into a Han-dominated political culture. (Farrer, 2014: 19)

This assimilation of minorities toward a Han culture is also demonstrated in terms of language. As Zhou (2003: 27) shows, 'In 1949, the percentage of Chinese-speaking minority people was probably below 20 percent... In the late 1980s, 50 to 60 percent of China's minority population could speak and understand Chinese... since the late 1980s China's market-oriented economy has greatly increased population mobility, both from minority communities to Han communities and from Han communities to minority communities. As more and more minority people speak Chinese as a second language or shift to Chinese as the first language and Chinese occupies more and more domains of language use, minority languages in China become less and less vital'.

Nevertheless, existing research has argued that the recent global economic change has provided new opportunities for the revitalization of minority languages through exploiting their potential economic and exchange value, in particular via heritage tourism. Heller (2003) approaches language from the perspective of the new economy wherein the economic restructuring and entry into the global market requires a re-evaluation of the multilingual repertoires in francophone Canada, and leads to the transformation of the development mode from workforce to wordforce (Heller, 2010: 353), or the entrance into a 'language industry' (Heller, 2010: 352). This strategy of 'globalizing nationalism ... abandons, in many aspects, the focus on nation-state institutions and searches for resources and power in international markets and institutions' (Pujolar, 2007: 82), and can also be found among other ethnolinguistic minority tourism sites (see e.g. Coupland *et al.*, 2005; Thurlow & Jaworski, 2010).

Though the francophone case may leave the impression that 'globalization can increase the value of otherwise minorized varieties' (Blommaert, 2003: 613) and may be 'the reason for the revival of local cultural identities' (Giddens, 2000: 13), such commodification of local language and identity materializes with conditions. As acutely pointed out by Heller (2003: 487–488), heritage tourism depends on 'the strength of the older ideology of community', because it 'combines the value of the authentic community with the development of a unique francophone product, of unique interest to francophones, and under francophone control'. This observation points to the importance of ideologies of language and culture as mediating factors between macrostructure and micro language practice. Thus, while the globalized new economy provides an opportunity for some minority people and their languages, others may have to resort to other strategies to enter the global market.

In the Chinese context, for instance, the language situation in ethnolinguistic minority groups is complicated by the stigmatization of minority languages, weak community participation in community development (see Bao & Sun, 2007) and the Chinese consumer culture, as mentioned above. For example, Bai (2001) describes the failed attempts by Manchu minority elites in northeastern China to revitalize their community as a tourism site through Manchu language education under the overwhelming promotion of Standard Chinese (Putonghua) and English learning. Pan (2005) examines the changing language attitude and language practice at the heritage tourism site Xi'an, which has led to the devaluation of the local Xi'an dialect, the changing attitude toward Putonghua as a lingua franca, the increasing desire to learn other dialects for better domestic tourism service and the frequent use of simple Japanese and English to serve international tourists. Su and Teo (2009), in their study of a heritage tourism site at Lijiang, observe how the local language is used for emblematic, decorative and authenticating purposes (such as dialect engraving on the wall), totally deprived of the communication function of the language (Blommaert, 2010: 29). What we see at West Street, Yangshuo, however, is not only the devaluation, if not erasure (Irvine & Gal, 2000), of the local language in tourism development, but more importantly the strategic use of English to establish itself as a 'global village'.

The second point I would like to make concerns the inflow of foreigners into China, in particular the changing attitudes toward foreigners in recent Chinese history. Farrer (2014) notes that

PRC [the People's Republic of China] attitudes towards 'foreigners' were also cast during this same period of state formation that emerged out of a long struggle against colonialism and foreign invasion. During the first half of the twentieth century many Chinese cities had gained substantial foreign populations, mostly located in semi-colonial 'treaty ports' such as Shanghai and Tianjin, or colonial possessions wrested from China, such as Hong Kong and Dalian. The new Communist leadership was determined to eliminate foreign political influences, expelling resident foreigners from the country in the early 1950s, or encouraging them to emigrate, including almost all long-term resident Westerners (and the last remaining Japanese) as well as Russians, stateless Jews, and other refugees still living in Chinese cities after the Communist takeover. Soviet advisers were an important exception to this cleansing of China's cities, but with the cooling of ties between the Soviet Union and China after 1956, they too were expelled, and previously multicultural (and colonial) cities such as Shanghai and Dalian became nearly devoid of foreign residents for most of the 1960s and 1970s. Beijing had a small population of diplomats and a few resident foreign communists, but even the capital city was scarcely a multicultural metropolis. (Farrer, 2014: 19–20)

The open and reform policy in 1978 ended decades of isolation for China and its people. However, 'in as much as Chinese did come into contact with foreigners inside China, the state worked to limit contacts to a polite facade of politically correct "friendship" [Brady, 2003]. These policies of restricting foreigners' entry to China, formed in a period of perceived national crisis, reinforced a psychological and social barrier between Chinese and foreigners that still impacts on intercultural relations today' (Farrer, 2014: 20). Early foreign travelers to China were often able to record the extraordinary attention they attracted from Chinese people – the 'staring squads':

The program is *Aliens*, you are the star, and cinema-sized audiences will gather to watch. You can get stared at in any Asian county if you have western racial features, particularly when you go off the beaten track where the locals have seen few or no foreigners. But China is phenomenal of the size and enthusiasm of its staring squads. …You don't have to do anything to get a crowd. Stop for a minute or two on the street to look at something and several local people will also stop. Before long the number of onlookers swells until you're encircled by a solid wall of people. (*Lonely Planet China*, 1994: 148)

Chinese people also have a term for addressing foreigners in general, 'laowai' (老外), which is arguably further evidence of how foreigners tend to be considered as outsiders:

Laowai! This is just an extension of the staring-squad problem. Laowai literally means 'old outside', but it's just a Chinese idiom for 'foreigner'. It is not a term of abuse – in fact it's the politest word for 'foreigner'. Nevertheless, it gets irritating, just as the words 'Hello Mister' in Indonesia begin to sound irritating after you've heard it for the 100th time in the course of 30 minutes. Just why the Chinese are so easily amused by standing next to a foreigner and repeatedly yelling 'Laowai' is hard to figure out – they must be very bored. (*Lonely Planet China*, 1994: 148)

While in both academic and popular discourses the intercultural experience between Chinese and foreigners is often said to involve such barriers, one social event, called the 'English Corner', has received relatively little attention, in particular with regard to how foreigners in such events have come to assume an instrumentally important role, rather than simply being laowai to be stared at.

The formation of the English Corner dates back to 1978, when China resumed English teaching after the Cultural Revolution. The first English Corner was formed at the People's Park in Shanghai. A place with many foreign travelers in China at that time, it quickly became the gathering place for people to find foreigners to practice their spoken English. Soon, practicing spoken English was widespread across China. Its proliferation was largely driven by the need to improve and practice spoken English beyond the classroom. Since the 1980s, almost every city in China has at least one free public place for weekly English Corners. Jin and Cortazzi (2002: 60) define an English Corner as 'a characteristically Chinese approach' to learning English: 'a weekly gathering in a park, a square or at a street corner where university and middle school students create their own learning environment with each other and passers-by, to practice English'. 'In most English corners, there is little organization and participants simply know that they can come and speak English to other learners at particular times. They may talk to complete strangers to make friends with people through practicing English together at will' (Gao, 2009: 61).

While an English Corner does not necessarily need to be held with foreigners present, the appearance of foreigners is now being advertised by language schools in Yangshuo as one of the important factors that differentiates them from other learning environments. On West Street, Yangshuo, a T-shirt (see Figure 1.3) from a T-shirt shop seems to allude to the fascination with foreigners, suggesting that (1) 'Thou shall not stare fixedly at foreigners', as well as cautioning against using foreigners for practicing English (see [8] 'Thou shall not utilize foreigners to practise English'). This new spin on interaction with foreigners is explored in Chapter 5.

In this section, I have provided a brief introduction to Yangshuo, situating the account within the changing ideologies of mobilities and tourism in contemporary China. I have shown that tourism mobilities constitute important aspects of the globalization process of China. While

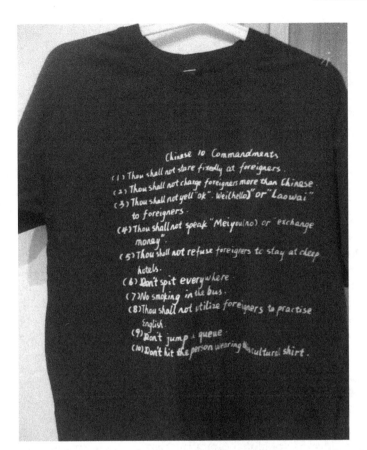

Figure 1.3 A T-shirt with 'Chinese 10 Commandments' (*Source*: Photo by author, 2011)

since 1978, international tourism has helped open China to the outside world, the socioeconomic change since the early 1990s has set China in motion, in particular through internal labor and tourism mobilities. Yangshuo, as one of the first places open to international tourists in China and a popular domestic tourism site, represents an important locale for examining how international and domestic tourism mobilities contribute to the reconfiguration of place, and how such transformation is related to the changing ideologies of language and mobility in an increasingly globalizing China.

In the following section, I discuss some theoretical concepts that help illuminate the sociohistorical change in Yangshuo. The purpose is not to provide a comprehensive review of the entire field of the sociolinguistics of globalization – there is scholarly work on this (see e.g. Coupland, 2010b; Kearney, 1995) – but to outline a conceptual framework that could help illuminate the present study.

Engaging with Globalization: Theoretical Considerations

Globalization

The term 'globalization' is often used to refer to this age of time–space compression that we are living in, and it is often said that the world has become a global village. However, sociolinguistically, as Blommaert (2010: 1) notes, 'the world hasn't become a village, but rather a tremendously complex web of villages, towns, neighborhoods, settlements connected by material and symbolic ties in often unpredictable ways'. In other words, this seemingly straightforward catchphrase 'global village' erases much complexity: varied material and semiotic processes are involved in the globalization process, which is often messy, complex, fluid and unpredictable (Blommaert, 2010, 2012; Coupland, 2010a). As a multifaceted empirical phenomenon, the meaning and significance of globalization also vary across society and shift according to individual's social, economic and political background (Garrett, 2010). Urry (2000: 12) attempts to summarize that there are basically five different, yet interrelated, perspectives, including globalization:

(1) as a strategy, as developed by transnational corporations;
(2) as an image used, for example, in commercial advertisements;
(3) as an ideology of global capitalism that argues for reducing the regulatory power of nation-states;
(4) as a basis for mobilizing individuals and organizations;
(5) as scapes and flows that involve the movement of people, money, capital, information, ideas and images through complex interlocking networks.

These perspectives, as I will show, are all relevant to the case of Yangshuo: the establishment of the 'global village' is both a strategy for local economic development and an image produced in tourism promotional discourses. This developmental process involves multiple tourism mobilities, which also serve as the basis for further strategic appropriation of certain flows, the English language and foreign backpackers in particular. And throughout this process of tourism development, private enterprises and investments are playing increasingly important roles in the commercial development of the local tourism industry. However, globalization is also a lived experience (Blommaert *et al.*, 2005), or simply 'banal globalization', as Thurlow and Jaworski (2010) suggest in relation to tourism. In other words, understanding globalization also means trying to understand everyday life events, real or imagined, through which people's understanding of and stances on globalization are materialized. In my analysis, I explore how various semiotic sources and different forms of mobilities are managed and experienced, by whom, for what and why. This leads us to a more detailed discussion of globalization below, drawing upon the concepts of mobility, locality and historicity.

Mobility and locality

In a number of publications, Urry (2000: 2) suggests that 'the material transformations that are remaking the "social", especially those diverse mobilities, ...are materially reconstructing the "social as society" into the "social as mobility"' (see also Hannam *et al.*, 2006; Sheller & Urry, 2006). As a discipline that can be roughly defined as the study of language in society, sociolinguistics is bound up with these changes in society. If the empirical phenomena we are observing are changing, as Blommaert (2010) notes, so should our analytical framework. 'A sociolinguistics of globalization', as Blommaert (2003: 611) suggests, 'is perforce a sociolinguistics of mobility' (see also Blommaert, 2010, 2012). He further elaborates that

> Mobility is the great challenge: it is the dislocation of language and language events from the fixed position in time and space attributed to them by a more traditional linguistics and sociolinguistics (the Saussurean synchrony) that will cause the paradigm shift that we are currently witnessing to achieve success. ... In order to get there, the notion of 'mobility' itself must be developed as well. (Blommaert, 2010: 21)

At the same time, globalization is also bound up with locality. As Blommaert (2010: 22) notes, 'mobility is the rule, but that does not preclude locality from being a powerful frame for the organization of meanings. Locality and mobility co-exist, and whenever we observe patterns of mobility we have to examine the local environments in which they occur'.

Here, I explain how mobility and locality are understood for the present purpose. Specifically, I address two aspects of mobility: language as a mobile resource (Blommaert, 2010: 9) and the differentiated mobilities of people (Massey, 1993: 61). I also show how mobility and locality are interconnected by discussing three understandings of locality, including the relationality of locality; locality, space and place; and locality and language ideology.

One way toward an understanding of language as a mobile resource is to differentiate between what Blommaert (2010: 5) calls the 'sociolinguistics of distribution' and the 'sociolinguistics of mobility'. The former sees the movement of language resources 'as movement in a horizontal and stable space and in chronological time; within such spaces, vertical stratification can occur along lines of class, gender, age, social status etc.', whereas the latter 'focuses not on language-in-place but on language-in-motion, with various spatiotemporal frames interacting with one another' (Blommaert, 2010: 5). Coupland (2010a) elaborates on this interaction of spatiotemporal frames in more specific terms. Drawing on Bartelson (2000), Coupland (2010a: 7, italics original) distinguishes among three ways of conceptualizing flows in relation to globalization: *transference, transformation* and *transcendence*. He notes that transference, 'the movement or exchange of things across pre-existing boundaries and between pre-constituted unites', constitutes the most established form of flows (Coupland, 2010a: 7). Specifically, 'demographic migration and the dissemination of cultural formats and products are straightforward examples of transference' (Coupland, 2010a: 7; see also Urry, 2000: 3). And the 'nothing new' argument regarding globalization (Coupland, 2010a: 7) can find its evidence in this sense of globalization as transference, notably in scholarly works on language contact (Coupland, 2010a: 10; see also Jacquemet, 2005: 260). Transformation, on the other hand,

> implies a more radical change, whereby flows modify the character of the whole global systems in which they function. Boundaries and units are themselves refashioned, as well as things flowing across and between them. In the third scenario, transcendence, 'globalization is driven forward by a dynamic of its own and is *irreducible* to singular causes within particular sectors or dimensions'. (Bartelson, 2000: 189, original emphasis; cited in Coupland, 2010a: 7)

It is this understanding of flows in terms of transformation and transcendence that informs the present conceptualization of language as mobile resources. More specifically, in the case of West Street, Yangshuo, the inflows of foreigners as well as the English language are not to be understood simply as movements across the pre-existing geographical area of Yangshuo in the sense of transference (Coupland, 2010a: 7); instead, these mobilities bring about concrete semiotic and material changes in West Street through transforming the space they are in and redefining the sense of place. Here, the English language acquires new meanings and significance, and constitutes an important resource in this transformation of a former neighborhood into a 'global village'. Language is therefore understood as a resource rather than a structural and autonomous system (Heller, 2010: 360–361), as being mobile and dynamic, 'framed in terms of trans-contextual networks, flows and movements' (Blommaert, 2010: 9), rather than being static and bounded. At the same time, the construction of the so-called 'global village' is driven by multiple interrelated factors, including not only 'a dynamic of its own', that is, the inflow of international tourists and the local economic restructuring, but also the changing ideologies of English and tourism mobility within the larger context of China. It is through this 'transcendence' perspective that I look at the transformation of Yangshuo at the nexus of local–national–global.

This then points to the importance of examining the language ideological processes through which languages are mobilized and enter into the local environment. As Blommaert (2003: 608–609) observes, the insertion of 'globalized varieties... into local environments' reorders 'the locally available repertoires and the relative hierarchical relations between ingredients in the hierarchy', creating 'newly stratified orders of indexicality'. And 'the key to understanding the process... is to discover what such reordering of repertoires actually means, and represents, to people' (Blommaert, 2003: 609; see also Pennycook, 2010: 6). The construction of a 'global village', as observed in Yangshuo, involves the mobilization of semiotic resources that are mediated by ideologies of language, that is, 'the cultural system of ideas about social and linguistic relationships' (Irvine, 1989: 255).

Here, Irvine and Gal (2000) provide the useful concepts of iconization, erasure and fractal recursivity to explore the semiotic processes for linguistic differentiation. They observe that 'it has become commonplace in sociolinguistics that linguistic forms, including whole languages, can index social groups. As part of everyday behavior, the use of a linguistic form can become a pointer to (an index of) the social identities and the typical activities of speakers. But speakers (and hearers) often notice, rationalize, and justify such linguistic indices, thereby creating linguistic ideologies that purport to explain the source and meaning of the linguistic difference' (Irvine & Gal, 2000: 37). The three semiotic processes are defined as:

Iconization involves a transformation of the sign relationship between linguistic practices, features (or varieties) and the social images with which they are linked. Linguistic practices that index social groups or activities appear to be iconic representations of them – as if a linguistic feature somehow depicted or displayed a social group's inherent nature or essence. This process entails the attribution of cause and immediate necessity to a connection (between linguistic features and social groups) that may be only historical, contingent, or conventional... *Fractal recursivity* involves the projection of an opposition, salient at some level of relationship, onto some other level... *Erasure* is the process in which ideology, in simplifying the sociolinguistic field, renders some persons or activities (or sociolinguistic phenomena) invisible. Facts that are inconsistent with the ideological scheme either go unnoticed or get explained away. (Irvine & Gal, 2000: 37–38, italics original)

In Chapter 3, I show how these semiotic processes work to create certain language ideologies that help to construct an image of the 'global village'.

At the same time, mobility involves not just the differentiation of linguistic resources, but also the differentiated mobilities of people (Massey, 1993: 61). People embodying valuable linguistic resources might be mobilized and used for the local purpose, which may result in changes in demographic makeup as well as unexpected ways of using and organizing space. This points to what Massey (1993) calls the 'power-geometry of space', which is how people are differentially positioned in relation to flows and movements. She notes that

this point concerns not merely the issue of who moves and who doesn't ... it is also about power in relation *to* the flows and the movement. Different social groups have distinct relationships to this anyway differentiated mobility: some people are more in charge of it than others; some initiate flows and movement, others don't; some are more on the receiving end of it than others; some are effectively imprisoned by it. (Massey, 1993: 61, italics original)

This observation of 'differentiated mobility' wherein some people might be 'imprisoned' (Massey, 1993: 61) echoes what Blommaert (2010: 154) calls 'soft marginalization': 'the marginalization of particular cultural features, identities, practices and resources such as language'. It is through understanding the dynamics and relationality among (im)mobilities that a sophisticated understanding of mobility can be achieved. In Chapters 4 and 5, I will show how English-speaking international travelers, embodying valuable English language resources, are mobilized for the local educational tourism industry, and how during the second wave of tourism development since the mid-2000s, tensions arise as to what West Street should be like and who should have control over and access to it.

Having established the understanding of language as mobile resources, and differentiated mobility, I now turn to locality. I have already noted the language ideological aspect of locality in relation to mobility. I will now further elaborate on the issues of the relationality of locality, as well as space and place.

Understanding locality requires understanding the relationality between the local and non-local. As Coupland (2003: 466) notes, 'even when our primary concerns are with sociolinguistic issues in particular locales (which is sociolinguistics' traditional ground), we need to address a range of factors linked to processes of globalization to account for these local circumstances'. This is because in the age of globalization 'attention limited to local processes, identities, and units of analysis yields incomplete understanding of the local' (Kearney, 1995: 548) such that local events need to be 'read locally as well as translocally' (Blommaert, 2003: 612; see also Leite & Graburn, 2009; Pennycook, 2010; Rampton, 2000).

This does not necessarily mean that locality should be understood from a defensive perspective. As Pennycook (2010) observes,

> to the extent that globalization is seen in terms of the homogenizing effects of capital expansion, environmental destruction, cultural demolition or economic exploitation, for example, the local becomes the site of resistance, of tradition, of authenticity, of all that needs to be preserved. (Pennycook, 2010: 3–4; see also Jacquemet, 2005: 263–264)

This presents just one way of understanding locality. As Massey (1994: 151) also observes, 'on this reading, place and locality are foci for a form of romanticized escapism from the real business of the world... "space/place" is equated with stasis and reaction', as shown in forms of 'reactionary nationalism' or 'introverted obsession with "heritage"' (see also Jacquemet, 2005: 261). In this study, I adopt what Massey (1993, 1994) terms 'a progressive sense of place', as she argues that:

> those writers ... frequently go on to argue that, in the middle of all this flux, one desperately needs a bit of peace and quiet; and 'place' is posed as a source of stability and an unproblematic identity. In that guise, place and the spatially local are rejected by these writers as almost necessarily reactionary. ...Perhaps it is most important to think through what might be an adequately progressive sense of place, one which fit in with the current global-local times and the feelings and relations they give rise to, *and* one which would be useful in what are, after all, our often inevitably place-based political struggles. The question is how to hold on to that notion of spatial difference, of uniqueness, even of rootedness if

people want that, without it being reactionary. (Massey, 1993: 64, italics original)

Massey (1994: 155) further suggests that there are 'a number of ways in which a global sense of place', that is, a sense of place that is 'extroverted' and 'integrates the global and the local', might be developed:

> First of all, it is absolutely not static. If places can be conceptualized in terms of the social relations which they tie together, then it is also the case that these interactions themselves are not motionless things, frozen in time. They are processes ...Second, places do not have boundaries in the sense of divisions which frame simple enclosures... it can come precisely through the particularity of linkage to that 'outside' which is therefore itself part of what constitutes the place.... Third, clearly places do not have single, unique 'identities'; they are full of internal conflicts: a conflict over what its past has been (the nature of its 'heritage'), conflict over what should be its present development, conflict over what could be its future. Fourth, and finally, none of this denies place nor the importance of the uniqueness of place. The specificity of place is continually reproduced... There are a number of sources of this specificity – the uniqueness of place. ... Globalization does not entail simply homogenization. On the contrary, the globalization of social relations is yet another source of (the reproduction of) geographical uneven development, and thus of the uniqueness of place. There is the specificity of place which derives from the fact that each place is the focus of a distinct mixture of wider and more local social relations. There is the fact that this very mixture together in one place may produce effects which would not have happened otherwise... all these relations interact with and take a further element of specificity from the accumulated history of a place, with that history itself imagined as the product of layer upon layer of different sets of linkages, both local and to the wider world. (Massey, 1994: 155–156)

It is this progressive and global sense of place that informs the present exploration of local and non-local dynamics. As I will show in Chapter 3, the so-called 'global village' in Yangshuo is not to be understood passively as an inevitable result of homogenizing globalization; rather, I show how the 'global village' is a social construct whose significance corresponds to the changing ideologies of English and tourism in contemporary China. And in Chapter 4, I show that there are tensions around the sociohistorical transformation, and yet such tensions are not to be understood in defensive terms as, for example, the loss of a former residential neighborhood; instead, I delineate the tensions around space in terms of the varied ways that different groups of people react to this social change and relate to each other.

This leads to the importance of understanding locality in terms of space and place (Pennycook, 2010: 3). In this conceptualization, locality is not simply understood 'in objective, physical terms' (Johnstone, 2004: 65) or just a context in the sense of a 'spatially fixed geographical container' (Sheller & Urry, 2006: 209). As Pennycook (2010: 7) suggests, 'the local needs to be understood in relation to a dynamic interpretation of space; ... local practices construct locality'. This study therefore adopts an understanding of place and space as below:

> What begins as undifferentiated space becomes place as we get to know it better and endow it with value ... the ideas 'space' and 'place' require each other for definition. ... Furthermore, if we think of space as that which allows movement, then place is pause; each pause in movement makes it possible for location to be transformed into place. (Tuan, 1977: 6, as cited in Cresswell, 2009: 4)

Specifically, I examine this issue of place and space in two ways. On the one hand, I explore the touristic construction of place from a process-based perspective (Harvey, 1993; Massey, 1994), looking at the sociohistorical processes through which the tourism site of West Street is developed as well as examining tourism promotional discourses to see how a certain sense of place is constructed semiotically and promoted. I will elaborate on this point below. On the other hand, I also examine the spatial dynamics, that is the potential 'in place/out of place' tensions (Cresswell, 2009: 5–6). As Cresswell (2009: 5) notes, 'the mapping of particular meanings, practices, and identities on to place ... leads to the construction of normative places where it is possible to be either "in place" or "out of place". Things, practices, and people labeled out of place are said to have transgressed often invisible boundaries that define what is appropriate and what is inappropriate'. This points to the importance of examining 'how the spatialities of social life presuppose (and frequently involve conflict over) both the actual and the imagined movement of people from place to place, event to event' (Hannam et al., 2006: 4; see also Massey, 1994: 155). I explore this issue in Chapter 4.

Historicity

I have so far discussed the issues of mobility and locality. Both, however, also need to be examined within specific histories. This is because 'mobility is something that has temporal as well as spatial features', such that 'even if features occur all over the globe, the local histories which they enter can be fundamentally different and so create very different effects, meanings and functions' (Blommaert, 2010: 24; see also Massey, 1994: 156).

Underscoring the issue of historicity is important for the present study in two ways. First, examining Yangshuo through historical lenses helps reveal the specific historical processes through which the so-called 'global village' is constructed in the first place. As Harvey (1993: 4) stresses, 'the first step down the road is to insist that place in whatever disguise is, like space and time, a social construct. The only interesting question that can be asked is: by what social process(es) is place constructed?'. Keeping this in mind helps us to understand the specificities of the local historical transformation, and the potential tensions and power relations involved in historical changes, thereby avoiding the pitfall of the often-deceiving image of global homogeneity caused by globalization (c.f. Blommaert, 2010: 140–144).

Second, historicity is also important for addressing the more specific issues of what particular activities and interactions mean for the people concerned. As Williams (1979: 276) observes, what occurs in a place is

Table 1.1 A brief summary of key concepts

Globalization	Globalization is a deeply contextual process that involves multiple and interrelated aspects: as an economic development strategy, as a projected global image, as an ideology for capitalist expansion, as the basis for mobilizing resources, as multiple scapes and flows (Urry, 2000: 12); as a daily experience (Thurlow & Jaworski, 2010).
Mobility	Language can be understood as mobile resources as opposed to autonomous structural systems (Blommaert, 2010: 5; Heller, 2010: 360–361; see Chapters 3 and 5). There is also the issue of the differentiated mobility of people as, for instance, in the mobilization of people embodying valuable language resources (see Chapter 5) and the 'soft marginalization' (Blommaert, 2010: 154) of people incompatible with entrepreneurship and mass commercialization (see Chapter 4).
Locality	The local appropriation of language is mediated by conceptualizations of 'social and linguistic relationships' (Irvine, 1989: 255), that is, language ideologies (see Chapter 3). Understanding locality also needs to address the relationality of local and non-local (Blommaert, 2003; Kearney, 1995; Pennycook, 2010; Rampton, 2000; see Chapters 3 and 5). Locality is also about understanding space and place (Pennycook, 2010) (see Chapters 3 and 4).
Historicity	Globalization is also a historical process (Blommaert, 2010: 24; Harvey, 1993: 4; see Chapters 3 through 5). Historicity is important for understanding the processes and dynamics involved in the production of local realities (Williams, 1979: 267, as cited in Harvey, 1993: 12; see Chapters 3 through 5).

not simply an event 'but the materialization of a history which is often quite extensively retracted' (as cited in Harvey, 1993: 12). The particular histories of China and its changing position in the world affect the way that specific cultural, spatial and linguistic practices acquire their functions and meanings. I have shown such historical contingencies in broad terms, discussing how mobilities and tourism acquire new social meanings for Chinese people in post-Mao China. And throughout my study, I constantly address how particular events and their significance are embedded in personal and social histories. A brief summary of the theoretical concepts is shown in Table 1.1.

Overview

This book is organized into six chapters. This chapter has briefly introduced the research site of Yangshuo, China. Contextualizing the recent transformation of Yangshuo in its local, national and global nexus, I show that understanding its recent social change requires addressing ideological, social and economic changes at larger scales. The tourism site provides an important venue for understanding the complexities and tensions in China's globalization process, as well as for addressing the sociolinguistics of mobility, theoretically and empirically. I also present a conceptual framework for the study by discussing the interrelated notions of globalization, mobility, locality and historicity.

Chapter 2 introduces the methodological issues and analytical focus. Based on online data and ethnography at the research site, I show how more specific research questions emerged during my fieldwork as well as explaining issues of field access, field methods and constraints on data collection. Three analytical perspectives are introduced by way of sharing ethnographic anecdotes, which point to empirical issues that will be explored further in the following chapters.

Chapter 3 looks at how the so-called 'global village' was established and in what specific ways it appeals to domestic Chinese tourists. Through examining tourism discourses, this chapter shows that the construction of the so-called 'global village' reproduces the changing ideologies of English as a status marker in a globalizing China. Nevertheless, it is also shown that tourists through their post-tourism writings position themselves in varied ways to this 'global village'. This commodified sense of place is negotiated by tourists as they activate and (re-)work the social meaning of place while performing their own identities. This highlights how place is a social construct, constantly transformed in the process of sociohistorical change, and also mediated by people's conceptualization, imagination and experience.

This transformation from a former neighborhood to a 'global village', however, is not without tensions. In Chapter 4, I explore how different social groups are involved and variously positioned in relation to each other in this historical process of dramatic change. Drawing on multiple data resources, I delineate a three-phase account of the historical transformation, and show that the so-called 'global village' actually consists of historically accumulated layers of mobility and mobilization, which co-exist in tensions. The meaning of 'global village' is highly contested, and the use of the 'global village' is in dispute, as shown in cases of shops moving away or closing down. It is argued that such contestation is grounded in tensions between the past and the present, the traditional countryside life and increasing commercialization, thereby showing the power of the 'global village' as a material, semiotic and discursive construct that can result in marginalization and exclusion.

Chapter 5 looks at English educational tourism. Through promoting the unique opportunity to practice English with English-speaking foreigners, English language learning has become an important part of the local tourism industry. I show the strategies of mobilizing English resources in the 'English Corner', that is, how foreign travelers embodying valuable English resources are mobilized by local language schools. However, contrary to the promotional image of a happy language learner practicing English everywhere in town, the actual stories of language learning are more complicated. Drawing on interview data with both language learners and foreigners in town, I show that language learners strategically manipulate interaction as they seek interactional opportunities, resulting in what I call 'interactional straining'. I suggest that such interactional practice constitutes an act of self-governing that is grounded in the valorization of English and the constant pressure for self-improvement in neoliberal China.

The final chapter provides a summary of the empirical findings and discusses the methodological and theoretical implications for globalization.

Notes

(1) In his paper on the sociology of tourism, Erik Cohen (1984) outlines four directions for tourism research, including tourists and their motivation; the relations between tourists and locals; the structure of the tourist system; and the impact of tourism.

(2) The freedom to move also comes with personal costs. While people's personal and social lives are no longer supervised by their danwei, the hukou system is still very relevant today for people's general social welfare. Relocating to and living in a place without a valid hukou of that place often renders one unqualified for the social welfare specific to that place, for example, in the areas of education and healthcare.

(3) Cited from the Chinese version of Wikipedia. See http://zh.wikipedia.org/wiki/%E5%B0%8F%E8%B5%84 (accessed 2 January 2014).

2 Approaching the 'Global Village'

As mentioned in Chapter 1, this study takes an anthropological approach to the 'global village' and examines it as a social field. The central concern is to understand its recent social transformation from the perspective of changing language ideologies and practices. More specifically, what factors contribute to the emergence of the 'global village'? What roles does the local government play in this historical change? Who are the tourists attracted by the 'global village'? What is the touristic experience like, for both domestic and international tourists? How do various groups of local people, e.g. local indigenous people and business owners, relate to this social change? What do they think of this social change, positively or negatively? How do they adjust to it? I would like to hear their voice. Obviously, addressing these questions requires engaging with multiple sources of evidence, and providing an 'iconic' (Blommaert & Dong, 2010: 85) description of the research site needs attention to the multiple mobilities, contingencies and complexities. In this chapter, I show how I approach the 'global village' from three analytical perspectives, drawing on online data and ethnography at the research site in 2011. As I will explain, it is an 'open-ended ... process of inquiry' (Blommaert & Dong, 2010: 1; Hymes, 1996: 7), which involves adjusting my understanding and revising my perspectives and questions. In explaining the research methods, I also share anecdotes from the field, which lead to empirical issues that I will explore in detail in the following chapters, including place-making and tourist identity, tensions of space and English educational tourism.

Discursive Construction of the 'Global Village'

Tourists seldom start out with no information on the journey ahead. 'Before the actual consumption of a particular tourist destination', as Urry (1990: 26) observes, 'potential tourists already have anticipated experience of the place through "non-tourist" practices, such as film, newspaper, magazines etc'. 'Without this discourse of publicity', Dann (1996: 1–2) also argues, 'there would be very little tourism at all'. In other words, tourism promotional discourses may have an impact on the way that people perceive place and carry out touristic activities. The first phase of data collection therefore makes use of news reports, tourism websites, tourist writings and guidebooks, as well as other historical documents/records available in library archives, so as to understand how the image of a 'global village' is constructed and circulated. It is worth noting at this point that this prior knowledge was both the company I kept (Heath & Street, 2008: 49) and also the claims I wanted to hold in check (c.f. Rampton, 2006: 388–389) during my fieldwork later.

The portrait of West Street as a 'global village' can be traced back to the late 1990s in both policy documents and tourism promotional discourses. While this period of time coincides with large inflows of tourists to Yangshuo, it would be a simplification to conflate such flows with globalization or the emergence of the 'global village', though these flows do constitute important material processes of social change. Through examining tourism-related discourses, in particular promotional discourses online, it is shown that these varied flows of people, materials and semiotic resources only acquire specific social meanings through a local process of meaning construction. Also, the popularity of the tourism site among domestic tourists indicates that other national factors must be at work as well. As I will explore in detail in Chapter 3, media discourses constitute important sources for constructing and promoting the image of the 'global village', which are meant to attract domestic Chinese tourists.

Who are the Chinese tourists targeted by such tourism promotional discourses? What kind of tourist roles are projected for tourists? And how do tourists themselves negotiate and perform their roles as tourists? Tourist writings online help provide important insights into these questions. A term repeatedly seen in these writings online is 'xiaozi', the closest translation of which is petit bourgeois. For some tourists, travelling to the 'global village' constitutes a form of consumption that bestows a certain degree of social distinction on them. Travelling, therefore, becomes 'a source of status' (Sheller & Urry, 2006: 213). Others, however, try to disassociate themselves from such a typical image of tourists as mere consumers of leisure. In Chapter 3, I will show how domestic Chinese tourists in their post-tourism writings take certain touristic roles and stances while positioning themselves in varied ways vis-à-vis the 'global village'.

I had also planned to follow tourist groups to West Street during my fieldwork, in order to gain a more concrete understanding of tourists: do tourists have preferences for certain kinds of shops or souvenirs? How do they interact with other people? (c.f. Jaworski & Thurlow, 2010). It was assumed that at least compared with individual tours, guided tours would be easier to follow as they are more organized, and tour guides would facilitate access to tourists whose stay tend to be temporary and transient. However, as I learned later, local tour guides always try to get commission from tourists' expenditures, so they do not normally guide tourists around West Street where many small shops are located. This was confirmed by my experience of asking for tourism brochures about West Street at the local tourism agencies. When I went to check whether there were any brochures for West Street, people would first give me a surprised look, simply reply 'no' and then completely ignore me. Guiding tourists to the countryside tends to be their regular business.

Online discourses thus provide otherwise unavailable data that allow me to examine how the 'global village' is discursively constructed and promoted, and how tourists negotiate their roles and stances in different ways. However, is the 'global village' as glamorous as it is promoted? How do people really get along in this 'global village'? The ethnographic fieldwork sought to find answers to these questions.

'What Do You Mean by "Global Village"?'

In the summer of 2011, I went back to Yangshuo for my fieldwork. My first impression on returning to West Street after five years was that it had become somewhat more commercialized. McDonald's and KFC had found their way to West Street. Located just near the entrance to the street, the KFC logo and the big yellow M stood obtrusively against the backdrop of karst mountains stretching far away. In the street, traditional buildings still housed little souvenir shops, coffee shops and restaurants, but there were more shops: a modern bakery store with landing windows, several shops selling branded handbags and luggage and quite a few nightclubs with fancy decorations. And while people still drank and ate at the tables along the street, the more or less uniform decoration and tidy layout of some restaurants looked much more businesslike than the casual family businesses I had seen in 2006.

I chose to stay at a little family hotel on Xianqian Road, which leads directly to West Street but is much quieter. After settling in, I first paid a visit to the Yangshuo Tourism Bureau to do some document research about the local tourism development. The bureau was about a 15-minute walk from West Street. However, compared with the renovated Qingming-style buildings on West Street, the office building seemed too shabby to be a governmental bureau. The walls were dark and peeling, the wooden doors were a faded green color and the windows were dusty. As I looked for the office of the head of the bureau, the names of the offices caught my attention. All the names ended with 'share of stakes' (股) instead of 'office' (室, 科 or 所) as is normally the case. It seemed to indicate that each office not only had charge of certain aspects of the bureaucratic responsibility, but also held corresponding shares in the relevant tourism revenue.

When I returned my hotel, I told the night porter about my observation. 'You see that hotel there?', he asked, pointing at a building opposite our hotel. It was a nice marble building with delicate wooden carvings on the front door and windows, unlike most of the surrounding residential buildings. It could be quite a fancy hotel, I thought to myself. Then it came to me that I had never seen people coming in or out of it. 'There is dispute', he explained. 'Several bureaus want to claim the property as theirs, but it cannot be decided whose property it is after all, so they just let it be a waste there until the dispute can be settled'. As it turned out, it was a matter of which bureau could claim the property and its management rights, and thus any business profits. In short, it was a matter of who had the rights to own it and make a profit from it. While I was already aware of the weak community participation in local tourism development (Bao & Sun, 2007), I was a little surprised that the government also had a vested interest in owning and managing some businesses here. This complicates the way the local government gets involved in the 'global village', and also, as I learned later, contributes to the tensions and struggles in this so-called 'global village'.

While collecting the written documents, I also visited local businesses to understand everyday life in this global village. Some of the businesses were names that I had read about online, some were introduced by my participants and local friends, and others were chosen by myself. The general principle was to gain an understanding of the various types of businesses in West Street and their relationship with this new representation of the 'global village'. I thus included coffee shops, hotels, travel agencies, bars and cafés (see Table 2.1 for details). For personal reasons, I did not research or visit nightclubs, where, it was rumored, illegal drugs were secretively sold, though I did explore their contribution to the tensions in West Street through indirect sources.

When talking with people, I always sought to find out how they related themselves to this place and its social change. Some peoples had no trouble in giving a positive answer, even cheerfully offering elaborations, being proud of it; some would look puzzled by my question – either repeating 'global village' slowly as they thought about it, or immediately

Table 2.1 Businesspersons interviewed

Business	Owner	Gender	Age	Place(s) of Origin[a]	Starting Year(s)[b]
Hotel	Henry	Male	52	America	2002
Coffee shop	Meng	Female	32	Guangxi	2003
Bar	Ding	Female	31	Henan (China), Belgium, Australia	2005
Restaurant	Yan	Female	39	Guangxi	2008
Coffee shop	Kay	Male	36	South Africa	2010
Travel service	Liu	Male	40s	Guangxi	1998
Coffee shop	Tian	Male	30s	Guangxi, Taiwan	2000/2010
Restaurant	Sun	Male	50s	Guangxi	1992/2010
Restaurant	Song	Female	30s	Guangxi, Singapore	1995/2007

[a]Several of these businesses were opened through partnerships, as indicated in place(s) of origin. All the interviews were audio-recorded, except the one with Sun.
[b]The last three businesses in the table changed locations later, as I will explain in Chapter 5.

returning the question to me, asking instead 'what do you mean, "global village"?'; and there were those who refuted me by immediately offering alternative labels, claiming that it's not a 'global village', but 'Wenzhou village' or 'Guangzhou village', terms that imply the recent demographic change and commercialization. These observations complicated what I had assumed before my fieldwork. My assumption was that the business owners may have decided to open their business here because of the expected economic returns from this 'global village', and therefore they liked West Street as it is; the local indigenous people, on the other hand, may have thought that the commercial development of the 'global village' meant the loss of their neighborhood, and would try to defend it against change in some way. However, as became clear during my fieldwork, the tensions around the social change cannot be understood as tensions between businesspersons and indigenous residents of the former neighborhood, or simply as tensions between hosts and guests or even the displacement of the locals. The increasing flows and the diversity of the population have made dichotomies like 'host–guest' less realistic. As Cohen and Cohen (2012: 2182) also note, '"Hosts" are frequently themselves "guests" in little developed destinations, wherein outsiders often engage in tourist businesses. Likewise migrant workers, guests themselves within a country, often also assume the role of host through casual employment in tourist enterprises' (see also Mavrič & Urry, 2009: 650). This is exactly the case in Yangshuo. Indigenous West Street residents are not 'hosts' to tourists; rather, business shops on West Street are run by people (foreign and Chinese) who have relocated to Yangshuo for varied reasons at different phases of the tourism development of the 'global village'. To understand the complexity of the social change and how people relate to it, we need to pay attention to the different trajectories and mobilities of people in this global village, as well as how they relate to each other in this process.

My understanding of the tensions around the 'global village' became much clearer when I noticed a protest paper on display. One day, while wandering around the street again, I saw a very eye-catching protest placard right in front of a hotel. I had noticed the hotel before, but it never caught my attention, like other hotels. However, the placard did say something: the hotel was protesting the construction next door. Henry, the hotel owner,[1] told me that a nightclub was to be built right beside his hotel. He already had enough of the booming noise from one nightclub operating on the other side of his hotel. Now, if this nightclub were built, his hotel could no longer do business – it would be noise from both sides. When he came to Yangshuo around 2000 from America, he chose to open a hotel because he liked it here, the beautiful scenery and the nice little neighborhood. But now everything had changed, worse than he could ever imagine. Asked what his plan was now, he said he was closing down. He could find no way to negotiate with his next-door neighbor because their construction had the approval of the local government, so why would they care? The placard read:

> As a private business, our hotel has always dedicated itself to charity work, donating about 650,000 Chinese yuan for the past ten years. Despite this, we now have to close our hotel because the Housing Construction Bureau has done nothing but destroying our peaceful life here. We thus had to close since 13 May. We welcome anyone interested to come in and have a look.

This eye-catching placard thus represented a last hope for Henry that it could help to whatever extent (Figure 2.1). I could clearly see that Henry's hotel was not only affected because of the construction noise, but also the entire adjoining wall on one side of the stairs was demolished.

Henry's case may seem like an exception or simply an incidental conflict initiated by a neighbor's business decision, which was supported by the government, and another individual's hotel. But Henry's indignation at being unfairly treated, if not brutally violated, and his general dislike of the current West Street resonated among other participants. The commonality among those who did not relate positively to West Street was that most of them had arrived in Yangshuo before its most extensive

Figure 2.1 Protest placard outside Henry's hotel (*Source*: Photo by author, 2011).

development around the mid-2000s, and now tended to choose to live away from West Street.

As I will show in Chapter 4, Henry's case, among others, sheds light on the complexities and tensions around space, and helps illuminate how these seemingly idiosyncratic and different perspectives toward the 'global village' could actually reveal the excluding power of the global village. I show how multiple groups of people are involved in the semiotic construction of place, and yet are differentially positioned at the various developmental phases of the 'global village'.

'You Are Here to Learn English, Aren't You?'

I had hardly arrived in Yangshuo, when I was repeatedly asked the same question, 'You are here to learn English, aren't you?'. While you can politely suppress your surprise at this unexpected question and say no the first time you are asked, you start to wonder what's wrong with them, or rather what's wrong with me, when the question keeps being asked. So, I decided to talk to the owner of the hotel I was staying in. She had asked me this very question when I first arrived. Cindy was Chinese Malaysian and spoke Mandarin. She had been running her hotel for about a year, but spoke with experience and observation. 'There are two types of people who would stay here long. One is those who want to learn English, another those looking for business opportunities'. Assuming that those learning English would be school students, I asked further, 'well it's not school vacation yet, are there students coming here to learn English?' 'Many English learners are not students', she quickly corrected me:

> 'They work somewhere else but still want to improve English. So they come. But speaking of schools, Some schools booked my rooms for their students last year, to learn English here [in Yangshuo]'. In a cheerful manner, she continued, 'the students are supposed to look for foreigners to have a talk in English, as an assignment, but they don't really know where and how they can do that. One day, Xiao Zhang [the cleaner at the hotel], overheard that the students were worrying about where they could find a laowai [foreigner] to talk with. She immediately pointed out, our hotel owner is a laowai! All the students then came downstairs to talk to me. Hahah'. (Field note, 11 May 2011)

Intrigued by this, I decided to look for a local language school to see how English learning takes place there. I started with well-known schools, as recommended by one local informant. The first few schools I visited would not allow me to do research *inside* the school itself. But when asked what kind of learning programs they provided for their students, all the schools suggested that I should consider going to bars, because 'we encourage the students to go to the bars; they can practice English there with foreign travelers'. One member of staff also provided me with a few names of bars.

Admittedly, going to bars would allow me to observe people talking; however, with people coming and going, it would be difficult to identify and approach students, and more difficult to interview them or record their conversation on the spot. So, I tried another two schools, and as luck would have it, I finally got permission from one school. This school, Samuel Language School, turned out to be one of the most popular schools among students, and was also one of the oldest foreign language schools in Yangshuo, with a history of around 10 years. Right outside the school building, there was a notice board with two impressive phrases: 'English Only' and at the bottom in smaller font 'success in English, success in life' (see Figure 2.2).

I went to reception and explained my intention, and very soon the manager walked out. 'Hi, what's your name?' he asked as he shook my hand. I was a little surprised that he spoke to me in English. I stumbled a little but nevertheless replied in English. He invited me to come to his office for a talk, again in English. After examining my research information sheet, he kindly offered that I could do my interviews, and also participant observation if I so wished. I thanked him as I walked out of his office, but I could not help checking with him, 'Are you Chinese?' 'Yes', he smiled and continued in English, 'we are supposed to speak English here – that's part of the requirement of the school; it's good for students. The same for you when you go around the school'.

Part of the reason they allowed me access was because the school has a VIP student learning program. This program is designed for students who sign learning contracts with the school for more than 28 weeks, thus automatically becoming VIP students. One privilege of being VIP students is that throughout their entire stay, they are entitled to three

Figure 2.2 'English only'; 'Success in English, success in life' (*Source*: Photo by author, 2011).

one-to-one individual interaction sessions with three different foreign teachers (though I am not). The purpose is to practice spoken English. The interactional content can be quite flexible, as long as it is appropriate for the students' English competence. Usually the school manager would have a tutorial template for the teacher, but the school permitted me to ask my own research questions.

The language of the interviews was English, of course. However, the students were from different English levels, ranging from Level 1 (introductory level) to Level 5 (advanced level) as defined by the school, so I tried varying the wording but still basically asking the same questions based on the students' language competence. At times, however, the students had difficulty understanding even repeated simple English, and I would then suggest using Chinese, to which no students objected. Altogether, I interviewed 24 students (aged from 22 to 40 years), each lasting around one hour. I asked questions about English learning inside and outside school, the reasons for coming to the school and others. Generally speaking, they were young working professionals (with an average age of 27.8 years), some of whom had no college degrees. They had held lower-rank professional positions in small or medium-sized enterprises dealing with international trade (see Table 2.2). But all of them had similar experiences of quitting or intending to change jobs before they came here, hoping that improving their English would help them find better jobs in the near future. The learning program at language schools in Yangshuo, which advocate improving English by talking with foreigners, is what attracted them here (see Extracts 2.1 and 2.2).

Extract 2.1

(Interview with Frank, 23 years old, works at Guangdong)

Shuang: What do you think is good about Yangshuo?
Frank: I think the most important one is West Street, West Street.
Shuang: West Street? Why?
Frank: West Street, yes. Because there are a lot of foreign travelers at Yangshuo. I think it's a good place to study English.

Extract 2.2

(Interview with Ted, 31 years old, works at Sichuan)

Ted: I have many chances to job hop, if I, if I, but my English is very bad, so I can't get this chance, if my English is well, I en, can success to job hop.

Table 2.2 Language learners interviewed (total number 24: 15 males, 9 females; average age: 27.8 years)

Name	Gender	Age	(Previous) job	Job location
Ted	Male	31	Production manager	Sichuan
Frank	Male	23	Salesperson	Guangdong
Dan	Male	24	Salesperson	Guangdong
Jon	Male	36	Salesperson	Guangdong
Mary	Female	27	Salesperson and HR	Guangdong
Lucy	Female	28	Housewife	Guangdong
Jake	Male	24	Business owner	Shanghai
Cindy	Female	28	Sales assistant	Guangdong
Scot	Male	31	Accountant	Inner Mongolia
Zed	Male	25	(Car) parts department supervisor	Hunan
Davis	Male	30	Electronic engineer	Guangdong
Amy	Female	30	Manager	Guangdong
Lora	Female	24	Logistics (planning to be salesperson)	Guangdong
Gregg	Male	26	Project manager	Jiangsu
Reid	Male	24	Typesetter (planning to do trading)	Hebei
Lilly	Female	28	Order processor	Guangdong
Lisa	Female	40	Accountant	Guangdong
Ali	Male	27	Business owner	Guangdong
Neil	Male	26	Salesperson	Guangdong
Tina	Female	22	Salesperson	Guangdong
George	Male	36	Project engineer	Guangdong
Helen	Female	22	Family business	Hubei
Alex	Male	27	Operation department (shipping company)	Guangdong
Carl	Male	28	Business owner	Guangdong

Shuang: You mean get another job, a better one?

Ted: I can get, I can get, maybe, er 20,000 yuan salary, but now I can't…. So I made a big decision to quit my job to study English for a long time.

Before the interviews, the students were told that the recorded interview was part of my research on English language learning in Yangshuo, and when I finished my questions, I allowed the students to ask any questions they had as a return of favor. The most common question

I was asked was how to study English well. While I did not have a ready answer, some students readily produced a notebook, jotted down my words and asked for the spelling if they were not sure.

The school also placed me in an orientation program, which involved observing several classroom lessons. This conveniently put me in touch with more people. As it turned out, I was not the only new teacher. One South African, one American, one Irish man and one Canadian were at the orientation with me. At this time of the year, with summer approaching, more students were about to arrive, and the school was starting to recruit more new teachers. Except the Canadian who had just opened a new business in Yangshuo, the other three foreign teachers were travelers and intended to teach for several months or longer (see Table 2.3 for a full list of teacher-interviewees). This English-teaching job would provide them with extra money for travelling, and it is also a very convenient way to get or extend their visa. The good thing for me as a researcher was that as I got to know these and other teachers better and I also got to know about the 'Western community' in Yangshuo. During their stay, many teachers had already formed some social network within Yangshuo, thus getting in touch with them offered me the convenience of getting to know about the foreign travelers and their life here.

Table 2.3 Teacher-interviewees (total number 7: 1 female; 6 males; average age: 30.7 years)

Name	Gender	Age	Nationality	Qualification	Language(s) spoken	Length of teaching[a]
Cathy	Female	29	American	BA	English	2 weeks
David	Male	41	American	MA	English	1.5 months
Jason	Male	27	South African	Diploma	English, Afrikaans	9 months
Philip	Male	25	Canadian	BA	English, French, Spanish, Chinese	1.5 weeks
Steve	Male	34	Irish	High school	English, Spanish	2 weeks
Sam	Male	28	South African	BA	English, Afrikaans	1 week
Peter	Male	31	American	BSc	English, Chinese, Japanese	1 year

[a]As I will elaborate in Chapter 5, because of their relatively long-term stay, the foreigners teaching English at local language schools are also called 'local foreigners' (本地老外) by local Yangshuo people. Length of teaching here refers to the time spent in their current teaching position in Samuel Language School till the time of interview. Three of the teachers, Steve, Sam and Peter, had taught in either Samuel's or other language schools in Yangshuo. Philip and Steve were working part-time, and others were full-time teachers. Except for Steve and Jason who traveled to Yangshuo for the first time and stayed, the other five teachers had actually been to Yangshuo before.

In Chapter 5, I will examine how language learners and English-speaking backpackers make sense of their interactions with each other. Tensions around talking to foreigners are revealed.

Summary

In this chapter, I have introduced the issues of research methods and analytical focus. Overall, based on data collected online and during field-work, the whole data set includes:

- online tourism promotional discourses;
- online foreign and Chinese tourist writings;
- on-site observational field notes;
- photographs of signage;
- interviews with West Street business owners;
- informal interaction with local people;
- participant observation and interviews at one language school for about one month;
- document collection/research at Yangshuo Library and Yangshuo Tourism Bureau, including books, videos, policy documents, news-papers and magazines.

I have shown stories from the field that have led to the analytical focus of the book, including place-making, tourist identity, tensions of space and educational tourism. I have mentioned the importance of examining the process of place-making, and noted that tourism promotional discourses have implications for the way tourists negotiate the meanings of tourism sites. The next chapter looks at the material and discursive processes of how the 'global village' is constructed.

Note

(1) All names (of people and schools) in this book are pseudonyms. English pseudonyms are used for English language learners despite their Chinese nationality (see Table 3.2). This reflects the school policy according to which they have to use English names.

3 Commodification of Place, Consumption of Identity: Making 'Global Village' a Brand

The presence of the English language and foreigners in West Street, Yangshuo, represents a 'semiotic opportunity' (Blommaert, 2010) for constructing a 'sense of place' (Gieryn, 2000; Johnstone, 2010), in particular for domestic tourists. This chapter focuses on the discursive construction of the so-called 'global village' based on an understanding of place in relation to globalization and mobility. In a country where learning English meant learning communist or Maoist doctrines (see Ji, 2004), and where tourism was cracked down on as capitalistic during the Cultural Revolution (see Arlt, 2008; Urry, 2002), it is desirable to examine deeper sociopolitical factors to find out how tourism and English acquired new social meanings and how that relates to the formation of a 'global village' in Yangshuo.

In examining the foregoing issues, it would be problematic to confine the analytical scope to the local community. As Philips (2004: 489) admitted, 'villages were treated by anthropologists as bounded at one time, even though we know this is an analytical strategy rather than the only reality'. On a related note, Rampton (2009: 700; 2010: 286–288; italics original) argues that 'when it comes to larger social change and political structures', looking '*within* rather than *between* or *across* communities [provides] limited explanatory power'. This is particularly true in the age of globalization when 'all places are tied into at least thin networks of connections that stretch beyond each such place' (Sheller & Urry, 2006: 209). Tourist destinations, moreover, function in a contingent system consisting of tourists, local people and their respective cultures (Leiper, 1990) wherein the 'fluid interdependence' (Sheller & Urry, 2006: 212) of factors on different scales form a global–national–local nexus (Su & Teo, 2009).

Drawing on these insights, this chapter problematizes a static, bounded and homogeneous understanding of place. First, language helps construct senses of place, which in turn can be commodified for structuring human experience (Johnstone, 2010: 10). 'Sense of place' refers to the attributes and qualities ascribed to a physical location and its semiotic-material components (Gieryn, 2000), thus language and discourse constitute important resources for place-making (see Johnstone, 2010). Second, place only makes sense through the subjective mediation and experience of place, such that 'physical spaces are sometimes designed with particular human experiences in mind' (Johnstone, 2010: 10). Third, the meaning of place could also be variously activated and negotiated through specific linguistic practices, pointing to the importance of examining the relationality between people and place through tourist discourses. As Pennycook (2010: 7) argues, 'our words are produced and understood in places that are themselves constructed and interpreted'. In talking about tourist destinations in particular, Sheller and Urry (2006: 214) observe that '[tourist] activities are not separate from the places that happen contingently to be visited. Indeed, the places travelled to depend in part upon what is practiced within them'. In other words, place acquires its sociocultural meaning not only because of its producers but also its consumers, who, in this sense, co-construct the sense of place as well. A tourist destination is thus interactively constructed, mediated by and subjected to the ideological interpretation of tourists. Hence, language as a social practice, or more specifically, 'a spatial practice' (Pennycook, 2010: 7), can be considered as a useful way to explore the issue of place.

In the following sections, I first provide an account of the sociohistorical factors leading to the observed development of West Street into a 'global village'. I then analyze two tourism promotional discourses and four tourist writings to explore the interconnectivity between people and place. I conclude by suggesting an understanding of the tourism site as a social construction wherein the social meaning of place is constantly constructed, mediated and even contested by, instead of only being a context for, tourist activities and behaviors.

The Recent Sociohistorical Transformation of West Street

After decades of social turmoil, China finally started to turn its attention to economic development with Deng Xiaoping's coming to power in 1978. The same year, the central government designated Yangshuo (Guilin) as one of the first few places open to foreign travelers. The domestic tourism market, on the other hand, remained largely non-existent, not only because leisure travel was unaffordable for the ordinary people, but also because it was socially sanctioned. Mobility was considered as undermining social stability and running contradictory to socialist doctrines (Nyíri, 2009; Su & Teo, 2009; Zhang, 2003). Up to the 1990s, China was largely an inbound tourism market for international travelers (Zhang, 2003).

To develop international tourism and facilitate tourist travel to rural villages, the Guangxi Communist Party initiated plans in the early 1980s to develop the Li River that flows through Guilin City, which would allow tourists to travel by boat and enjoy the beautiful scenery all the way from Guilin to Yangshuo (*The Tourism Industry in Contemporary China*, 2009: 137–138). West Street, located on the west bank of the Li River, was the first place where foreign travelers disembarked after hours on the river. As more travelers arrived to explore the beauty of the countryside, residents on this 500-meter-long street started to open Western food restaurants and small family hotels catering to foreigners. Other local residents searched their backyards for typical Chinese products for sale, or did carving, painting and calligraphy writing on the street, catching the eye of foreign travelers who were amazed with anything Chinese. Through business services and self-learning, local residents were able to pick up some foreign expressions, e.g. Japanese and English, enough to serve travelers from neighboring and Western countries. Yangshuo's beauty quickly made it a popular tourism site, and by 1998 it had already become 'one of those legendary backpacker destinations that most travelers have heard about long before they even set foot in China' (*Lonely Planet China*, 1998: 774). West Street, the only street in the county with hotels and restaurants, also became a resting place for foreign travelers after exploring the surrounding countryside and villages. Its atmosphere is well captured by a Canadian tourist:

Extract 3.1

Yangshuo is unlike any other place we have seen in China to date – one entire section of the town seems like it has been lifted from somewhere else and plunked down in the middle of southwestern China. Cafe after cafe offering western food, espresso, capuccino [sic], pizza, real French baguettes, Italian gelato, and apple pie. Shop after shop with beautiful things from all over southern China from batik work to silk pyjamas [sic]. You could enjoy one English-language movie over dinner and stay for the double feature over dessert. (Parlow, 2001)

This transformation of West Street is such that it looks 'unrecognizable' to people who visited there in the early 1980s:

Extract 3.2

The pictures of West Street came as somewhat of a shock to me. When I went to this lovely place in 1984 there were less than 3–4 foreign tourists. No signs were in English. I stayed in an unpretentious room in a hotel with a central courtyard. Dinner was taken in a poorly lit restaurant where I sat for many hours holding the owners [sic] baby in my lap as I simply relaxed and watched the family. There were bikes for rent and I went with a friend to the countryside for an afternoon. I met another traveler who was out too late one day to get back to town, so a family took him in. He slept in a large bed with the entire family under one big blanket. From the pictures on this site it looks like this place has become yet another 'hip' tourist trap. It is completely unrecognizable. I am glad I went when I did. (Leach, 2004)

It would be a simplification, however, to consider the transformation of West Street as westernization driven by globalization, though international tourism does contribute to the observed change. As will be demonstrated in the next section, in its attempt to explore the domestic tourism market, West Street is no longer just a geographical location for Western food, but has acquired a new social meaning – 'global village'.

West Street as Brand: English, Tourism and (Post-)Modernity

As Yangshuo (and West Street) enjoys growing popularity among foreign travelers, tourism in China has also acquired new significance and meaning after decades of sociopolitical constraints and ambivalence. From the early 1990s, particularly after the Asian financial crisis, the central government started to heavily promote domestic tourism as it tried to encourage consumption to boost the economy (Zhang, 2003). Three-week-long holidays (Labor Day, National Day, Spring Festival) were introduced in 1999, aiming to 'truly make tourism a part of the people's common consumer practices' (Nyíri, 2010: 62; Zhang, 2003). These new policies and propaganda aimed at creating new subjectivities among Chinese people toward leisure, consumption and tourism; in the end, they helped Chinese tourists gain a widespread reputation as 'big spenders' (Nyíri, 2010). Tourism thus represents not only leisure, but also a 'quest for modernity' (Wah, 2009: 72), in particular among the increasing number of middle-class Chinese (see also Arlt, 2008; Nyíri, 2010).

In this national turn toward a consumer economy, the Yangshuo Tourism Promotion Committee was established in 1999, and a series of policies and projects were initiated to share this burgeoning domestic tourism market. The initiative began with the 'West Street Protection and Development Project' in 1999 that, while aimed at restoring the historical architectural style of West Street already popular among foreigners, can be considered a precursor of the more extensive commercial construction of a 'global village' that took place later. Generally speaking, the renaming of West Street as a 'global village' was an attempt to construct and commodify a sense of place. While English was mainly used in West Street as a tool of communication for service encounters with foreign travelers, the local government[1] now started to reframe the presence of English as an 'opportunity' (Chen, X., 2009: 80) that needed to be explored further and appropriated as one of the resources for constructing a sense of globality for Chinese tourists. To understand this strategy, the social significance of English among Chinese people needs to be introduced.

In the late 1970s, the English language was reintegrated into the national education policy for China's modernization (Pride & Liu, 1988). However, the current social importance assigned to English has gone beyond national development and international communication, to become a social stratifying factor within society. For one thing, with the further implementation of a market economy in Deng's China, English has become an unequally distributed educational resource, making English learning more of a market-driven activity. English is also learned as a school subject through formal education, and has a high stake in entrance examinations from secondary level to postgraduate studies. Consequently, English competence and education level are to a large extent mutually indexical – English competence could be one indicator of one's ability and social status (Zhao & Campbell, 1995). However, equalitarian distribution and access to language education resources proved hard to implement in China, given the regional differences socioeconomically on the immense landscape of China. More importantly, with the further implementation of a market economy, foreign language education started to be decentralized and pragmatically differentiated according to each region's specific socioeconomic reality (Hu, 2005), which made language learning more of a personal responsibility and investment. For another, English in China has a high value in people's upward social mobility (education, employment and others). While this overemphasis on English has always been a hot topic of debate, as one social critic famously questioned: '我们Chinese 总不能拿英语互相问路到长城怎么走吧?' (Shall we Chinese use English to ask each other which is the way to the Great Wall?),[2] English nevertheless has become a key index of personal competence and social status (Jin & Cortazzi, 2002; Zhao & Campell, 1995), leading not only to the nationwide craze for English, but also to critical self-evaluation of Chinglish or Chinese English (see Henry, 2010). English, as a marker of prestige and cosmopolitanism, has therefore become a necessary or desired part of the stylistic repertoire of many Chinese people.

Against this social background, the local Yangshuo government started to capitalize on English and develop West Street as a brand, as illustrated by a local official in an article titled 'The soft power of culture in Yangshuo tourism development':

> The tourism industry could be most developed when it is well integrated with cultural elements. Tourism development is actually a process of producing, managing, and selling culture, to be followed by tourists buying, enjoying and consuming culture. West Street, Yangshuo ... has become the largest English Corner, the 'Global Village' in China ... West Street offers its tourists super value services more than worthy of this brand. Culture development thus should follow the steps of tourism development: cultural products can become commodities, as highlights and brands of the tourism industry. (Chen, J., 2009: 172–173)

This branding strategy was implemented through two interrelated projects. The first concerned the development of an English education industry through building on the English-speaking environment in West Street. With the initiation of the English Summer Camp in 1998, 'educational tourism' was promoted as a new tourism attraction for Chinese nationals who wished to learn/speak English in an 'authentic' environment. As one official stressed in his article 'Promoting Yangshuo: Towards a scientific development of the County's economy':

> We should fully explore the opportunities of mixing Chinese with western cultures by strategically integrating more western elements into local Yangshuo culture. This would include importing educational resources from both home and abroad, so as to further expand and develop the foreign language education as an industry. (Chen, X., 2009: 80)

Building on the presence of foreign travelers, and based on the teaching philosophy of encouraging students to practice what they learn in the classroom by talking with foreigners, private language schools started to proliferate, and English language training became an important part of the local tourism industry (see Chapter 5 for details).

At the same time, building on the popularity of West Street among tourists, the local government also decided to further expand and establish West Street as a 'global village'. In 2003, with the 'West Street Protection and Development Project' still underway, the government initiated projects for the commercial development of real estate surrounding West Street. Favorable investment policies were issued, which were meant to attract private business investors from China and abroad.[3] To further promote and celebrate a 'global' image, the local Yangshuo Tourism Bureau started to organize cultural activities such as beer festivals and Christmas parties on West Street every year. This image became such an important part of the county's self-presentation that in 2005, a Frenchman who ran a restaurant on West Street was invited by the local government to be the spokesperson for Yangshuo (Liu, 2005).

West Street is now not just a place for international travelers to take a break, but it has also become a 'global village' where aspiring middle-class Chinese tourists can try out stylistic repertoires. Today, people from neighboring provinces and cities, Guangdong in particular, literally consider Yangshuo their 'backyard garden' in which to spend the weekends. In summer, West Street is a popular place for people from different parts of China to practice their spoken English. Part-time and unpaid volunteer working positions at hotels, bars and cafés even become opportunities only available on a first-come basis due to the sheer number of people eager to talk to foreigners through this 'convenient' means. While the popularity of West Street benefits the local businesses to some extent, the ideology of English symbolism also brings a dilemma: Not only is the street now losing its tranquility, but business owners and foreign travelers sometimes find themselves caught up with domestic tourists and English learners, who are eager to strike up an English conversation but usually with no clear communicative purposes.

In this section, I have shown that the transformation of West Street from a traditional residential neighborhood into a 'global village' involves the reframing of English as one of the semiotic resources to be mobilized and appropriated for constructing a sense of globality for domestic tourists. These developmental projects, however, are at the same time complemented by various discourses on tourism promotion. Indeed, as mentioned in Chapter 2, producing various discourses of publicity constitutes an important part of tourism development. The local Yangshuo government explicitly specifies that 'advertising and promotion constitute important aspects of tourism development... In terms of specific methods, we should rely on ...various tourism meetings and events, and also use the modern multimedia technologies of television and internet ...to promote in multiple channels and multiple forms' (*A Fast-Developing Tourism County*, 1999: 46). The following section thus examines two promotional discourses where this image of a global village is produced and promoted.

Semiotics of the 'Global Village'

The following extract, quite a typical introduction to West Street, is from the travel section of www.china.com.cn, which is a general information website under the supervision of the Information Office of the State Council. This article appears in Chinese in the travel information section, and is intended for domestic Chinese tourists. Similar introductory texts can also be found on many other information websites and travel forums.

Extract 3.3

Yangshuo has picturesque scenery and rich cultural heritage. …The most famous is the ancient stone street, West Street, which has many craft shops, calligraphy and painting shops, hostels, cafés, bars, and Chinese kung fu houses. It is also the gathering place for the largest number of foreigners – more than twenty businesses are owned by foreigners. So the place is called the 'Foreigner Street'. And since all the locals can speak foreign languages,[4] it is also called the 'Global Village' [Chinese original: 地球村]. …Another attraction is the study and exchange of Chinese and foreign languages and cultures. …Chinese people teach their foreign friends Chinese cultures including its language, calligraphy, taiji, cooking, chess; at the same time foreigners teach Chinese people their languages and cultures, so that both finish their 'study abroad' within a short time. (West Street, 2001)

The article, entitled 'West Street, Yangshuo: Heaven for xiǎozī' (xiǎozī 小资, to be explained later), introduces West Street as a 'Foreigner Street' (yángrén jiē 洋人街) after briefly describing its geography and history. While this name foregrounds the presence of foreigners and thus helps create a sense of Otherness, as I will demonstrate below, it is only introduced to be reframed for the construction of locality.

Through highlighting (Bucholtz & Hall, 2005; Park, 2010a), if not exaggerating, foreign languages as part of the local linguistic repertoire ('all the locals can speak foreign languages'), foreign languages are appropriated recursively (Irvine & Gal, 2000) to transform Otherness into locality. This sense of locality is then further constructed as globality – foreign language competence is linked in a causal relation with the notion of 'global village' – thus both establishing and naturalizing foreign languages as an index of globality. Through these semiotic processes, Otherness is thus transformed into localized globality. This recursive move becomes more evident when the author likens coming to Yangshuo with 'studying abroad', which differentiates West Street from the rest of China.

What is important, however, is not only the semiotic construction of the global village, but how tourism discourse, as Leiper (1990: 17–18) sharply points out, serves as the ideological positioning of tourists (see also Bruner, 1991: 248). Based on a presumably transient ('within a short period of time') and synthetic friendship ('foreign friends', 'Chinese friends'), Chinese people are encouraged to participate in an exchange of languages and cultures, which are represented as accessible and pleasurable. Here, it is important to note how this touring experience can become a symbolic performance for constructing certain tourist roles. West Street, as indicated in the title, is supposed to be the heaven for xiǎozī, who can be said to be the cultural role model in modern Chinese society, in particular among the younger generation. As either a noun or an adjective, xiǎozī refers to (a persona characterized by) a cultured and studied way of being under consumerism and hedonism (Bao, 2002), capturing qualities that may include:

> Non-mainstream and elusive uniqueness, which shows a surrealistic and romantic contemplation of life by displaying observable nostalgia, solidarity, educatedness, sophistication, elegance, usually in place and space with western associations like coffee shops and bars, so as to find a way of being and a sense of self in a post-modern spirit.

Xiǎozī thus tend to

> challenge and change everyday mundaneness into aesthetic and artistic experience, through travelling, clothing, furnishing, romantic love, etc., as exemplified by their preferences for movies (e.g. *In the Mood for Love*; *Sleepless in Seattle*), people (e.g. Zhang Ailing; a street beggar reading *Norwegian Wood*, see Bao, 2002), cities (e.g. Beijing, Shanghai), music (e.g. jazz, blue, folk) and others.

The tourism site of West Street, Yangshuo, as we see in Extract 3.3, provides opportunities for tourists to engage with the West, including the opportunity to meet and interact with foreigners, relax in bars and coffee shops, try Western food and others. Through these consumption and interactional practices, tourists exhibit their tastes and lifestyles that, as we shall see in the next section, might carry the connotations of being xiǎozī. In particular, one specific language indexical of xiǎozī is English, an indispensable element of the middle-class stylistic repertoire. In Extract 3.4, West Street is promoted as the largest English Corner:

Extract 3.4

Yangshuo is a good place to cure your 'dumb English' [Chinese original: 哑巴英语] and 'deaf English' [Chinese original: 聋子英语]. ...At West Street, you can always see West Street people talking in fluent English with western travelers for business or just having small talk. Even old grannies in their 70s or teenage kids can chat [Chinese original: 拉呱láguǎ] with laowai in English. Many western travelers say they just feel no foreignness here. West Street is the largest 'English Corner' in China now. (Yangshuo Tourism Bureau, 2009)

The article begins by invoking linguistic insecurity among Chinese people with the popular terms 'dumb English' and 'deaf English', which refer to inadequately developed English-speaking and -listening competence respectively. Such stigmatization of ordinary Chinese people's English is legitimated and justified by taking an authoritative stance with the clinical metaphor 'cure', which endorses West Street as the ideal place to improve English competence. Such linguistic authority is further attested to by depicting English as already being a natural part of the local linguistic repertoire (as indicated by the characterization of speaking English as 拉呱 láguǎ, a colloquial and laid-back style of conversation), and also by citing Western foreigners' judgments for credentials (c.f. Park, 2010b). While this seems to suggest that English might already be part of the local linguistic repertoire, and even that a language shift might be happening here, an evaluation of language competence is always situated and ideological (Blommaert et al., 2005; Park, 2009, 2010a, 2011). Indeed, during my fieldwork, I never heard the local people chitchat, or láguǎ, in English among themselves. Additionally, quite a number of people, staff and owners of businesses, told me that they spoke little or no English at all. As Song, a restaurant owner, told me,

I speak little English myself, and so do my staff. You cannot require them to know a lot [of English]. It's fine that they only know a little bit English words. If you want people with good English, you will never be able to find someone to work for you. Those people speaking good English would be competent enough to work in big cities in Guangdong or Shanghai. (Extracted from interview)

Nevertheless, while the locals may not really láguǎ in the manner the text describes, the English language, as well as the presence of Western travelers, occupies a significant part of Yangshuo's self-presentation. And such constructed language competence and authority, while questionable, have been quite successful due to mediatization in attracting Chinese tourists, who not only come to polish their English but also to witness the locals' linguistic achievements. An elderly woman living in Moon Hill Village in Yangshuo County became a national celebrity after it was reported that she could speak as many as eight foreign languages. Domestic tourists not only attempted to strike up an English conversation with her, but they also took photographs with her. Later, in a national television interview, she admitted that she had only picked up a few simple foreign expressions (Yu, 2005).

In this section, I have shown that the 'global village' image in tourism discourses is constructed through the semiotic processes of recursively appropriating linguistic and cultural resources, naturalizing their indexicality as globality and establishing linguistic authority. Such discursive construction fits into and facilitates the tourism developmental strategies adopted by the local government since the late 1990s, and has implications for the way that potential tourists perceive this 'global village'. So, how do tourists align themselves with such discursive strategies of attracting tourists? The next section examines tourist discourses online to find out how they position themselves in relation to the 'global village'.

Performance, Stance and Tourist Identity

Tourists, through their discursive practice, may activate the indexical meaning of various symbolic resources in West Street and thus position themselves in relation to the image of the 'global village' (Jaffe, 2009). The indexicality of English as xiǎozī, however, can also be subjected to negotiation. As has long been recognized in tourism studies, 'participants in a performance do not necessarily share a common experience or meaning; what they share is only their common participation' (Bruner, 1986: 11), thus 'referring to the tourist … is unrealistic' (Leiper, 1990: 17, originally underlined). Based on an understanding of identity as positioning oneself through linguistic practices (Bucholtz & Hall, 2005), I show two different stances that tourists take on the 'global village': post-tourists and anti-tourists. While the former explicitly embrace West Street as the wonderland for styling oneself as xiǎozī, the latter distance themselves from such a stereotypical image in various ways.

Post-tourists

The post-tourist, according to Jamal and Hill (2002: 94), is 'a sophisticated traveler who enjoys ludic experiences … The visitor participates in an illusory, hedonistic consumption of signs, symbols and images where the aesthetic experience rates higher than capturing the "authentic" original. In this postmodern scenario, accumulating aesthetic and culturally driven experiences becomes a game of achieving status, distinction and "difference"'. One such tourist is 'A cloud in the heart' (2005), a registered member of lvping.com, a website under China's largest travel service company Ctrip. Her excitement at having been there is expressed in a 10,000-word travelogue 'Xiǎozī life in Yangshuo, Guilin', which describes in great detail each day of her travels by inserting exclamation marks and symbolic tokens of English. A few have been extracted as follows:

Extract 3.5

The bus stopped at the entrance to West Street. Here it is. The legendary West Street, right now in front of us. Yet, I did not feel fully prepared to say to it '*Hello! Nice to meet you*' (para. 6)

That's the best position to take a picture of the Elephant Trunk Mountain, so here robbed us of our numerous *feelings*, hahah. (para. 18)

[Coffee shop name] has comfortable sofas and good coffees. The music is good, too. After we came in, many people as xiǎozī as us also had their seats. We just indulged there for the whole afternoon. I guess a real xiǎozī life is just like this. I can't love it more!! (para. 76)

After a detailed account (470 words) in Chinese of her pre-trip preparation and flight to Yangshuo, switching into English at the first sight of West Street is a marked choice of code. On the one hand, it signals a change of semiotic space, thus foregrounding the foreignness of West Street and setting the scene for her later use/choice of English. On the other hand, the personification of West Street through greeting indicates an evidently positive stance on the place, setting the tone for a happy touring experience. This English greeting thus serves as a metapragmatic frame, or a 'key to performance' (Bauman, 2011: 711), both setting the stage (West Street) and introducing the performer (the author). The following discourse thus involves enthusiastically switching into English as a stylistic resource, projecting an image of a fun-loving tourist (e.g. para. 18). This construction and performance of identity becomes more evident in a coffee shop. Here, the author both assumes and identifies with the xiǎozī identity ('many people as xiǎozī as us') by 'indulging' in coffee, which represents middle-class taste in a traditionally tea-drinking country (see Bao, 2002; Simpson, 2008). But since performance of identity can always be subjected to evaluation or even contestation (Bauman, 2011; Bell, 2011), a sense of insecurity was countered by reflexively authenticating oneself as xiǎozī ('I guess a real xiǎozī life is just like this'). Thus, in seeking to maximize the acquisition and exhibition of xiǎozī stylistic resources, 'A cloud in the heart' (2005) positions herself as a post-tourist who enjoys West Street as the so-called heaven for xiǎozī.

Since performance as 'virtuosic display' always requires 'creative exercise of *competence*' (Bauman, 2011: 709, italics mine), we could also expect to see how knowledge of performance can transform into discourse *for* self-management (c.f. Gershon, 2011: 542–543; Jaworski & Thurlow, 2009: 209–210). As will be shown below, performance of identity in West Street also occurs at a higher level of reflexivity, wherein tourist discourse becomes both the discourse of performance and the meta-discourse of performativity.

Extract 3.6 is written by Bamboo, who introduces himself/herself as an experienced xiǎozī tourist, claiming that 'if you follow my advice, you will never be ignored in Yangshuo' (para. 2). This expert stance is constructed by appropriating the genre of guidebook: the title *Guide for being xiǎozī in Yangshuo* metapragmatically schematizes his/her personal experience and observation into authoritative expert advice (Bauman, 2011: 711). The guide is neatly organized into three sections 'Preparation', 'Sight-Seeing' and 'West Street Life', each containing specific suggestions on stylistic resources for distinction, including clothing (para. 5), trip planning and transportation (paras 6–7), restaurants (paras 8–14, 17, 19) and displaying cultural and symbolic capital, such as flipping through English books and talking with foreigners (paras 14–16; para. 19). Thus, in attempting to stylize other tourists, the author simultaneously positions himself/herself as an experienced and superior post-tourist and reproduces Yangshuo as a place only for people with xiǎozī aspirations. This assumed tourist-ship (and readership) is actually clearly indicated right at the beginning by pointing out the need to pay attention to identity and language:

Extract 3.6

Identity

It would be best of course if you are a laowai or a mixed-blood [born to parents with different nationalities]. But since this guidebook is not for laowai, so let's just forget it. Putting that aside, you should come from

Guangdong and it's better if you are from Guangzhou or Shenzhen [two large cities in Guangdong province], being a white collar with xiǎozī experience or expectations. Besides, you may also come from Beijing or Shanghai, which are also places full of xiǎozī. Yangshuo welcomes those people.

Language
You must hold a CET-4 certificate,[5] with relatively fluent spoken English, because at West Street, or just at countryside farmhouses of Yangshuo, even an old grandma or an egg-seller from a rural family could surprise you with their amazing English and at least another foreign language. Next of course you should know Cantonese, kind of an official language here, 'cause more than half of the xiǎozī are from Guangdong. The third comes Putonghua, better with Beijing accent. The local dialect just does not work there. (Bamboo, 2002)

In these two points, the author maps a relationship between language, place and identity, yet in a rather non-essentialist paradigm, implying that what matters is not identity in the demographic sense, but how language can be employed as a stylistic resource to enact coolness and cosmopolitanism. This expert post-tourist stance is strengthened by prescribing an 'order of indexicality' (Blommaert, 2007b), with fluent English topping the hierarchy as a 'must' and local dialect being silenced (c.f. Bruner, 1991; Thurlow & Jaworski, 2010) as useless. However, the author not only indicates their superiority by giving expert advice, but also demonstrates this self-claimed xiǎozī identity through their own linguistic practice (e.g. 'Of course I would go with banana pancake or other fruit cakes, egg rolls, plus *Coffee*, *Milk* or *Juice*. Enjoy a western breakfast can be so cheerful and luxurious'. Para. 14, not extracted). Thus, in presenting their touring experience as a guide, Bamboo not only projects a post-tourist identity, but also sets themselves as the very referee (Bell, 2011) for other tourists.

Anti-tourists

We now turn to a different stance. There are also anti-tourists who focus on 'the expected or perceived shallowness of experience of place within traditional tourism, [with] a tendency to condemn superficiality', thus distinguishing and distancing themselves from other tourists (McCabe, 2005: 91–92). The following extract is from 'West Street, Yangshuo: Loss and Indulgence' by *nowherekid*, which appeared in the travel section of the popular website Sina.

Extract 3.7

We've read many travelogues about West Street. It's said that West Street is not just a place for a tour – it should be lived and enjoyed. So we spent most of our week living there. West Street is actually a place for hedonism, where you can forget everything and just indulge yourself. The most popular? Bars and foreigners... Our best memory about West Street was sitting in an open-air café, just watching people come and go, aimlessly killing the afternoon ... And at a *bar*, after writing many words, I left with satisfaction and fulfillment... So that's why people love here. From the perspective of a xiǎozī, it's true that Yangshuo is a good place, a habitat for your soul... But I would not consider myself a xiǎozī, and feel no good about the label... The heaven for xiǎozī can be a hell for me sometimes... Things here are overcharged... the highly commercial atmosphere is disgusting... As it is, Yangshuo today no longer needs painter Xu Beihong, or National Father Sun Wen. It's just where you can be xiǎozī, lose yourself, and indulge yourself. (*nowherekid*, 2010)

The way that *nowherekid* consumes the symbolic resources through coffee, English and bars in West Street resembles most post-tourists – she actually both anticipates and acknowledges that she might be taken as another xiǎozī tourist by just being in Yangshuo (e.g. 'From the perspective of xiǎozī, it's true that Yangshuo is a good place, a habitat for your soul'). Nevertheless, she attempts to differentiate herself from such a stereotypical image by explicitly denying the indexicality ('But I would not consider myself a xiǎozī'). Thus, while being a co-participant in the global village with post-tourists, she reconstructs her touring experience and thus her identity by taking a moral stance against both West Street and xiǎozī tourists. She criticizes its commercialization and condemns other tourists for their ignorance of the sociohistorical and political importance of Yangshuo. Xu Beihong (1895–1953) is one of the greatest painters in modern China, and Sun Wen (better known as Sun Yat-sen, 1866–1925) is the founder of the Chinese Nationalist Party. Both had spent some time in Yangshuo. Yangshuo County still preserves the former residence of Xu Beihong, and has established a statue of Sun Wen in the square where he made an influential speech. These two places are within a few minutes' walk from West Street, but are seldom mentioned or visited by other tourists. In adopting an anti-tourist stance, *nowherekid* therefore simultaneously distances herself from post-tourists and positions herself as a more sophisticated tourist with sociohistorical concerns.

Reservations about West Street as a global village for xiǎozī are also shown in less explicit but more critical ways. 'Brother Big Horse' has a blog entry at Sina, one of the most popular blog sites in China. The article, humorously entitled 'Travelling fugue at West Street: Suggestions and Strategies', begins with a parallel of propositions: 'West Street is the heaven for xiǎozī. If you come to have fun, you should be a xiǎozī; if not a xiǎozī, then a xiǎozī-to-be; if not a xiǎozī-to-be, then pretending you are xiǎozī' (para. 1). While it sounds like the author intends to provide helpful suggestions based on his 'close observations of xiǎozī in West Street so as to play it real' (para. 4), his actual advice, mostly concerned with language use, turns out to be subversive parodies:

Extract 3.8

1. No real names. You need to get a foreign name using the 'bird language' [鸟语niǎo yǔ], better with about four syllables. It sucks if you call out 'hey, brother'.
2. Don't drink tea or juice. Drink coffee. Tea, or juice, that's just being lame. How elegant drinking coffee is! …
3. While talking, even if you speak Guilin dialect, remember to insert several bird words. Two cautions: choose familiar words and pronounce the bird language in a pure and standard way; another is pretending to speak casually and effortlessly.
5. Be crazy! Even with the slightest fun, say 'yě' [野]! …
8. Expressway to being a xiǎozī. Order coffee at tea houses. But don't you say 'give me a cup of coffee!'. Say gently 'kāo fēi' [尻绯]! (Brother Big Horse, 2006)

Using foreign names, a seemingly most accessible strategy to construct a xiǎozī identity, is considerably undermined when the author renames English the 'bird language', a term used among Chinese people to flag language crossing (Rampton, 1995), implying that the language makes no sense. This illegitimization (Bucholtz & Hall, 2005) of English, therefore, not only subjects post-tourists' linguistic practice to ridicule, but also rekeys the author's advocacy for longer ('four syllables', maybe thus sounding more sophisticated) English names as quite sarcastic. This anti-tourist stance is further shown in his seemingly pompous comments on coffee (Point 2) and wine (Point 3, not extracted), the symbolic resources favored by xiǎozī. His satire toward the post-touristic linguistic practices continues in Point 4. By hypocritically reminding tourists of the issues of word choice and manners of articulation, he hints at the ill-at-ease efforts that post-tourists make when trying to sound fluent and natural, indicating the possibility of failed attempts by either overshooting (Bell & Gibson [2011], so 'speak casually and effortlessly') or undershooting (Bell & Gibson [2011], so 'choose familiar words'). Such performance failure actually becomes the target of the author's sarcasm later. By deliberately mistranscribing 'yeah' as '野' (yě) and 'coffee' as '尻绯' (kāo fēi), while the correct Chinese equivalents would be '耶' (yè) and '咖啡' (kā fēi), respectively, the author re-indexes the use of English as irrational '野' (yě) and nonsensical '尻绯' (kāo fēi). Thus, under the guise of giving voice to post-tourists, the author subversively exposes their linguistic practices in a highly stylized manner, transforming post-tourists from being the subject/agent of performance to the object/target of ridicule, through which he has been able to metalinguistically criticize such performance as pretentious, illegitimate and irrational, thus distancing himself as an anti-tourist.

The above analysis shows that tourists, through their discursive practices, position themselves in relation to the semiotics of place, align themselves with other tourists and, at the same time, reproduce or reconstruct the social meaning of place in varied ways. Tourist discourse, therefore, serves as an important site where the contradictions and tensions surrounding the indexicality of English, the identity performance of Chinese tourists under consumerism and thus the reservations about the global village image are being worked out.

Understandably, post-tourists and anti-tourists, as introduced here, are not meant to be exhaustive categorizations of all tourists to West Street, Yangshuo. Instead, it shows how tourists adopt different tourist roles during their touristic consumption while displaying varied levels of reflexivity and taking different stances on each other and the global village. While post-tourist discourses reproduce West Street as a place for accumulating stylistic resources to construct a xiǎozī identity, for anti-tourists such identity performance only represents superficial touristic consumption to be criticized and ridiculed. The anti-tourists, as we have seen, position themselves in varied ways to the 'global village'. Their contestation is established through negatively evaluating the tourism site and other tourists, thereby positioning themselves as being more sophisticated and knowledgeable. Through showing their cultural and historical awareness ('painter Xu Beihong, National Father Sun Wen' *nowherekid*, 2010) and mocking the pretentious and erroneous use of English by post-tourists (Brother Big Horse, 2006), anti-tourists seem to indicate that the touristic significance of the 'global village' corresponds to people of a particular social class and taste, which more sophisticated and knowledgeable people may not conform with or may even hold in contempt.

Summary

In this chapter, I have explored the issue of place by examining the construction of a 'global village'. I have shown that the process involves not only material processes of tourism planning and development, but also discursive construction of the image of place in the media. Specifically, I have shown the semiotic processes in which the English language is appropriated for commodifying a sense of globality for domestic tourists in tourism promotional discourses. To understand this sociohistorical process, I have argued, requires going beyond locality in our analytical scope and beyond a static and objective understanding of place, to consider the convergence of various sociohistorical factors at a global–national–local nexus (Su & Teo, 2009). In the present case, the observed commodification of place occurs in the context of a national turn toward consumerism, wherein English acquires the functions of social stratification and tourism becomes a modern consuming practice. The 'global village' is thus neither simply a geographical location nor a product of westernization, but a social construct whose significance corresponds to ideologies of language and culture at wider national levels.

It has also been shown that understanding tourism sites requires exploring the interconnectivity and contingency between people and place, because tourist activities and behaviors constitute an integral part in (re-)producing, mediating and negotiating the meaning of place. Globalization challenges an objective and bounded understanding of place not only because of the mobility of symbolic and material resources across space, but also because people are both on the move and positioned to move. As Sassen (2002: 2, as cited in Hannam *et al.*, 2006: 7) notes, the mobility of resources always involves 'pronounced territorial concentrations of resources necessary' for managing mobility. This study shows that West Street is commodified as a global village through mobilizing and concentrating semiotic resources into one geographical location so as to mobilize people by promoting certain tourist roles. In this sense, semiotic resources are mobilized both for constructing locality and for channeling mobility.

It is worth noting that English, as one important stylistic resource for constructing a xiǎozī identity, only represents one part of the stylistic repertoire of tourists, and identity performance always happens in multimodal environments (Bell & Gibson, 2011). As the analysis shows, coffee shops and bars are relevant spatial resources as well. It is the indexicality that the English language affords in combination with other semiotic resources that makes the xiǎozī experience both possible and desirable.

At the same time, it has been shown that the construction of tourism sites also involves tensions because of tourists' varied conceptualization and imagination of place. The touristic experience does not happen passively in a presumably given geographical location. Rather, tourists through their discursive practices reflect on the relationality between their behavior and place, in terms of the meaning of the touring experience, their relation with other tourists and their stance on the place. The contestation and negotiation of the touristic meaning of the 'global village', in particular by anti-tourists as we have seen, indicate that there are class- and taste-based tensions around what the 'global village' means. The next chapter further explores the contested nature of the 'global village', shifting the perspective to the local dynamics of space.

Notes

(1) The commercial development of West Street is a governmental initiative, instead of a community decision, as in Heller's case (see Bao & Sun [2007] for a discussion on the weak community participation in Yangshuo).

(2) This critique was made by Han Han (1982–), one of the most influential writers and social critics in contemporary China. The specific source of his remark can no longer be traced, but it is included in the online Chinese Wikipedia Baidu Baike as one of his many famous words. See http://baike.baidu.com/view/5972.htm (accessed 21 February 2012).

(3) Non-local capital is recruited for two reasons. First, as a countryside village, both the local people and the government lack the financial capital for investment. Second, it also h elps attract foreign businesspeople for the construction of a global image. See Chapter 5 for details.

(4) The original Chinese version does not indicate the number of 'foreign language' [外语wàiyū] or specify which language(s). 'Foreign languages' is thus used as the translation in a general sense.

(5) CET-4, abbreviation for College English Test (Band 4), is a national English exam, and a prerequisite for gaining a college degree from many universities.

4 Tensions of Space: Living on the Margins of the 'Global Village'

Ten years after the West Street development project, voices of concern have been raised about the developed West Street. One local official noted that:

Extract 4.1

There are now challenges for West Street. West Street has been expanded, but it has also undergone changes in its outlook, which means it is now attracting different customers. The street used to mainly offer leisure activities for international travelers. But later, large numbers of domestic tourists come as well, because they want to take a look at the 'Foreigner Street' and experience western ways of living. Therefore, the current West Street has added some extra attractions for domestic tourists, which means West Street could no longer be the same. This would have negative effects on the future development of West Street. We should recognize that, the reason West Street has become so famous and attract so many domestic tourists is because it has been attracting international tourists in the first place. And yet don't forget the reason why West Street attracts international tourists is because they can enjoy the traditional leisure culture here. (Chen, X., 2009: 81)

The concern is not only from the local government. During my field-work as I talked to my participants, foreign and Chinese, they critically reflected and commented on how they liked and lived around West Street and Yangshuo. So exactly who are the people living there now? What kinds of touristic businesses are there? What changes have taken place in the ambience of West Street? And have such changes caused problems for the people living in the 'global village'? To address these issues, I will map out the demographic, linguistic and geographic changes to West

Street, and then explicate the specific ways that people adjust and relate to a fast-changing place.

However, I should stress that I do not seek to pinpoint where and what is 'wrong' with the tourism development, or offer practical solutions or suggestions for future tourism planning and policy of Yangshuo – that is beyond my ability and was never my intention to do so. Instead, my objectives in this chapter are to (1) explain and demonstrate through historical lenses how the construction of the 'global village' involves the reorganization and differentiation of space by different businesspeople; and (2) map out some of the current local dynamics arising from this sociogeographic and demographic change. I will engage with these issues by looking at mixed evidence from:

• policy documents and demographic data;
• interviews with businesspersons and local foreigners;
• field notes and observations;
• linguistic and semiotic materials, including signage and language use.

These data provide complementary insights into the historical change and current local dynamics in varied ways: policy documents and demographic data help produce official and statistical accounts from the perspective of tourism planning and development; interviews, field notes and observations bring in local perspectives; and signage and language use provide insights into West Street as a space of transformation (e.g. Blommaert, 2012; Stroud & Mpendukana, 2009; Stroud & Jegels, 2013). In their call for a material ethnography of linguistic landscape, Stroud and Mpendukana (2009: 363) define 'landscapes as semiotic moments in the social circulation of discourses (in multiple languages), and view signs as ...socially invested distributions of multilingual resources, the material, symbolic and interactional artifacts of a sociolinguistics of mobility'. Blommaert (2012: 46) also suggests 'see[ing] signs as material forces subject to and reflective of conditions of production and patterns of distribution, and as constructive of social reality'. Adopting this materialist perspective enables us to examine 'how space is semiotized, and how it semiotizes what goes on within its orbit' (Blommaert, 2012: 29), and more importantly, how it could potentially contribute to our understanding of the dialectics among signs, practices and people (Blommaert, 2012: 59) and 'the situated social dynamics of multivocality in local places' (Stroud & Jegels, 2013: 2).

I should emphasize here that I can only hope to provide a partial – if there is such a thing as full knowledge (c.f. Blommaert, 2012: 12; Hymes,

1996: 13) – picture of the tensions around the sociohistorical change of Yangshuo during the past three decades. And in synthesizing this mixed evidence, I adopt a narrative-descriptive approach as suggested by Yi-Fu Tuan (1991), a humanistic geographer, who observes that 'all narratives and descriptions contain at least interpretative and explanatory strata-gems, for these are built into language itself'. He further elaborates that:

...a theory, by its clarity and weight, tends to drive rival and comple-mentary interpretations and explanatory sketches out of mind, with the result that the object of study – a human experience, which is almost always ambiguous and complex – turns into something schematic and etiolated. Indeed, in social science, a theory can be so highly structured that it seems to exist in its own right, to be almost 'solid', and thus able to cast (paradoxically) a shadow over the phenomena it is intended to illuminate. By contrast, in the narrative-descriptive approach, theories hover supportively in the background while complex phenomena them-selves occupy the front page. For this reason, the approach is favored by cultural and historical geographers, historians generally, and cultural anthropologists – scholars who are predisposed to appreciate the range and color of life and world. Their best works tend to make a reader feel the intellectual pleasure of being exposed to a broad and variegated range of related facts and of understanding them a little better (though still hazily), rather than, as in specialized theoretical frameworks, the intel-lectual assurance of being offered a rigorous explanation of a necessarily narrow and highly abstracted segment of reality. (Tuan, 1991: 686; see also Rampton, 2013: 5–6)

This chapter develops as follows. I first provide a three-phase his-torical account of the 'global village', delineating the local demographic, semiotic and spatial transformations, focusing more on the two waves of tourism development during the past decade. I show how this historical process of development results in the redefinition of space alongside prac-tices of mass consumption and entertainment. I then propose a descrip-tive typology of space of the current 'global village', suggesting how the different touristic businesses on West Street represent different ways of organizing space that affect the way that people relate to and live around this 'global village'. There are *spaces of privacy*, *spaces of transaction* and *spaces of sociability*. Then, I focus on businesspersons and local foreign-ers, the two major groups of people living in this 'global village', to see how they relate in varied ways to this fast-changing place. I examine this by looking in particular at how spaces of sociability constitute key sites of spatial differentiation and friction. I explicate that different styles of sociability, arising partly due to tourism business investments and mass commercialization, are manifested sociogeographically in this 'global village' in two ways. First, I show three cases of moving away and one case of closing down, that is, how three businesses had moved away from West Street into quieter streets nearby, and how in one case a hotel was struggling over closing down. I also outline the tensions around the (mis) use of space in these relatively quieter streets, which are local foreigners' niche of sociability. This also sets the scene for Chapter 5. I conclude by arguing that the 'global village' is not a space of free mobilities and flows, but a space of power that excludes and marginalizes some social practices while facilitating, if not cultivating, others.

The Changing Landscape of the 'Global Village'

In this section, I provide a historical account of the demographic, semiotic and spatial change of West Street, focusing more on the first (late 1990s to early 2000s) and second waves (mid-2000s to 2011) of tourism development. At the end of this section, I provide a summary table of these changes (see Table 4.1, p. 85).

Till the late 1990s: A laissez-faire West Street

West Street used to be a residential street in Yangshuo, a multi-ethnic county populated by 11 ethnic groups including Zhuang, Yao, Hui, Miao, Tibetan, Dong, Korean, Tujia, Manchu, Bai, with the majority (87.4%) being Han. The official languages of the county, as elsewhere in the Guangxi Zhuang Autonomous Region, are Standard Chinese and Standard Zhuang. Each ethnic group is said to have its own ethnolect(s). The Han people are speakers of different Chinese language varieties. The Hui people also use the Chinese language, but they have borrowed vocabularies from Arabic due to their religious practice of Muslim. The other ethnic groups have their own ethnolects and corresponding writing systems.

No historical statistical data are available on the demographic makeup and language use on West Street per se, but according to the official statistics in 1988,[1] the most commonly used Chinese languages among Yangshuo people in general are Yangshuo dialect, used by more than 90% of the population; Hokkien, used among early immigrants from Guangdong, Fujian, Jiangxi, Hunan and other provinces; and boat people language[2] (船家话 chuánjiā huà or 蜑家话 dànjiā huà), a sub-variety of Cantonese used among boat people (also called Tanka people, a derogative term) who make a living from fishing. But most people are said to be able to speak or understand Standard Chinese (*Yangshuo County Chronicles*, 2003: 412–416). Apart from these Chinese language varieties, the Zhuang language[3] is supposed to have the second largest number of speakers since the Zhuang people are the second largest ethnic group in Yangshuo (more than 10%). No existing academic research, however, can be found on the use of the Zhuang language, or ethnolects in general, in Yangshuo. And the very few studies into the use of the Zhuang language in other areas of Guangxi have produced mixed results, perhaps partly due to the large geographical distribution and variation of the Zhuang people and their languages. During my fieldwork, I got to know two Zhuang people, in their late twenties and early thirties, respectively. Neither is distinguishable from the Han people in appearance, costume or even language. One is Meng, the owner of a coffee shop on West Street. She moved to Yangshuo from another city in Guangxi and told me that she is half Zhuang, because her mother is Zhuang and her father is Han. She claimed to speak a little bit of Zhuang. The other is a tour guide from Yangshuo. According to him, even his grandfather cannot speak Zhuang. The only trace of ethnolinguistic diversity, as I observed around West Street, is reflected in the bilingual signboards of official institutions. Variously located within about 5–20 minutes' walking distance from West Street, all official institutions are linguistically marked in both Zhuang letters and Chinese characters (see Figure 4.1), with the police station bearing a third language of international communication – English (see Figure 4.2). Apart from these signboards of official institutions, the Zhuang language is nowhere to be seen around Yangshuo.

While the ethnolinguistic diversity of West Street is difficult to trace, the start of tourism in the late 1970s seemed to prompt the use of English among early business owners. Some started to use bilingual signboards. According to Wang's (2006a) historical research into West Street, Meiyou Café was one of the early private businesses, opened by a Zhuang girl from southern Yangshuo. She initially named her café 'Ping', a character from her given name. However, tourists, foreigners in particular, were always disappointed by the fact that her restaurant did not have much to offer. Wang (2006a) recorded that

> When foreigners came and asked 'do you have beer here?' She told them 'meiyou' [a Chinese word in pinyin, meaning 'don't have']. 'How about Italian pizza and Mexican burritos?' 'Meiyou'. 'French champagne and salad?' 'Meiyou'. 'Then you have nothing here', the foreigner teased

Figure 4.1 'Yangshuo County Library' in Zhuang (above) and Chinese (below)
(*Source*: Photo by author, 2011)

Figure 4.2 'Police Station' in Zhuang (top), Chinese (middle) and English (bottom)
(*Source*: Photo by author, 2011)

Figure 4.3 Meiyou Café (*Source*: Reproduced from *An Intoxicating West Street* (2007[2004]: 84))

her. But gradually she learnt about what the tourists need for food and drinks, and also learnt to make them. She then with the help of friends made a cartoon style bilingual signboard and changed the name of her shop to 'meiyou café' [see Figure 4.3]. This caught the eyes of passers-by and she was able to make a big success. (Wang, 2006a: 129–130)

However, not everyone was as lucky as Ping. According to Yan, who had a restaurant on West Street since 1995, 'there were not as many restaurants with western food. Even in the 90s, there may be only less than ten such restaurants. It was not easy to buy the ingredients for western food'. Additionally, coming from the planned economy, people had to learn to do business through trial and error, and it was not unusual to hear of people losing money from investing in businesses (Wang, 2006a). Nevertheless, some shops started selling traditional cultural products. Wang (2006b) recounts when the very first antique store on West Street, 'Xiao Jin-Ge', opened up and had an eye-catching golden character signboard:

In the mid-1980s, there were not many business shops. Some houses had brick walls and were renovated with windows so as to be used as living rooms or for housing tourists. The owners of the shop Xiao Jin-Ge paid a monthly rent of 60 yuan for a room of more than 30m² to sell antiques. At that time, there were tourists from Western Europe, Japan, and also Taiwan. Every noon, more than 100 ships and boats would stop by the east dock, and these tourists would step on to West Street. …One day, a tourist from Taiwan… said to the owner of this very first antique store: 'Mr Zhang, there are many foreigners on this street and you have very good business, but why don't you have a sign board? With a sign, people recognize and remember you, and can come for you or even introduce businesses to you'. The couple then decided to pick one character from each of their given names, and named the shop Little Jin-Ge (小金阁 xiǎo Jīn-Gé). During the Spring Festival that year, Mr Zhang heard that a famous calligrapher was helping residents with spring couplets[4] at the People's Hall. So he went to ask the calligrapher to help him write the three characters '小金阁'. He then found a wooden board at home, placed the characters on board, and spent three days carefully carving out the three characters as exactly. (Wang, 2006b: 590)

Other local people knew about drawing, painting, calligraphy and seal carving and began to sell these products. Liu, a travel service center owner, told me that in the 1990s, he would occasionally visit West Street. His girlfriend, now his wife, was a resident on the street. At that time, he was working as a secondary school teacher of mathematics in his hometown nearby, but he also had a great interest in drawing. So later, he started drawing and selling T-shirts while also learning to speak English for business interactions in the process; finally, he resigned his job to work as a tour guide in Yangshuo.

During this period, West Street was largely a residential street, though there were a couple of souvenir shops and restaurants for tourists. The development of West Street was left to chance. As Liu told me, 'the local government did not care much about our business. Yangshuo did not have as much publicity in the 90s. The government did not try to get enough publicity, nor had clear plans to develop any tourism sites'.

First wave of development: 'Global Village' and 'English Corner'

From the late 1990s, some businesspersons from home and abroad gradually started to settle down in the neighborhood. Tian, who claimed to have opened the very first coffee shop in Yangshuo in 2000, recalled what West Street was like back in 2000:

Extract 4.2

Most people, they just searched their backyards for old wooden boards or 'ancient' stones, and sold them. That's it. Those kinds of old stuff, which looked like ancient treasures. Hahaha. They were just not sure about what they should sell except that the foreigners might be interested in this kind of stuff'. (Extracted from interview)

It was also around this time that tourism started to gain increasing importance in the local economic development, in a turn to a 'tourism-based economy'. Apart from the socioeconomic change within the larger context of China (see Chapter 3), several local factors also contributed to this turn toward tourism, including the recognition of the importance of the tourism industry for local economic development, and the privatization of the economy. First, the privatization of the economy was triggered not only by the burgeoning market economy, but also by the reduction in national and regional subsidies for economic development. This meant that the local government had to assume more autonomy and independence in seeking financial resources, relying more on private investments. As one government official said,

As has already been pointed out by the Regional Communist Party, no more state-owned business enterprises will be approved in any County and levels below. This means that our future economic development has to rely on the existing public economy, and yet at the same time we need to seek out new developments through non-public economies. We should break away from the outdated dichotomy between the so-called 'public' and 'private', and establish an ideology where private and public economic forms are equally recognized ... To achieve this, we need to first create a favorable environment for fair business competition, abolishing the outdated regulations and rules set against private and individual business forms; second, warmly welcome non-local non-public enterprises, including foreign businesses; third, supporting existing private and foreign business.... (Guo, 1999: 22)

Second, in this time of financial and economic structural change, the local government began to attach great importance to the tourism industry as a key contributor to the local economy. As one local official argued:

There are still many problems in our tourism development: the development rate has been slow, the overall quality is not good enough, tourism resources have not been well explored, and the whole industry is not yet systematically organized and managed. This will affect the future of tourism development ... The main reason for these existing problems is that we have not yet fully recognized the importance of the tourism industry. It is true we have been engaging in tourism, but we have never considered it seriously, which thus constrains the development of tourism and use of tourism resources. Therefore, we must first of all reach a new understanding of tourism so as to further develop it. We must recognize that tourism is an economic industry with a large demanding market. And more importantly, it requires relatively fewer investment capitals and yet brings quick economic returns. This is a great advantage compared with other industries... Moreover, the tourism industry is a comprehensive industry and its development could also bring about development in related industries. It could not only provide a large market for agricultural, industrial and other business products, but also help stimulate the development of transportation, communication, food industries, and entertainment. (Zhao, 1999: 45–46)

It was also specified that:

...tourism should be developed as the leading industry of the local economy. ... The ultimate objective is that for the next five-year plan (1998 to 2003), the average annual growth rate of the tourism revenue should be more than 16%, aiming for a total annual tourism revenue of more than 250 million Chinese yuan in the year 2003. The added value of the tourism industry should account for more than 50% of that of the tertiary industry. (Guo, 1999: 19–20)

Meanwhile, it was stressed that developing the tourism industry 'requires a departure from the old production-based development ideology to one focusing on circulation, flows and service' (Tan, 1999: 31–32). The local government also decided that tourism forms needed to diversify 'from only scenery tourism to be expanded to include culture, agriculture, exploration, entertainment, and learning' (Tan, 1999: 33), including English language teaching, as we shall see in detail in Chapter 5.

It is against this local context that some new businesses started to appear on West Street. Not far into West Street, for instance, there is a very large French restaurant, LeVotre (see Figure 4.4), opened by the spokesperson for Yangshuo who was introduced in Chapter 3. He had been staying in Yangshuo since 1993 and opened his restaurant in 2001 (Liu, 2005). It is said that he has managed to cooperate with tourism agencies in France and they have been sending about 10,000 French tourists to his place each year (Liu, 2005).

Figure 4.4 樂得法式餐廳 LeVotre Restaurant (*Source*: Photo by author, 2011)

In this early phase of development, the former residential neighborhood with family businesses was gradually changed both demographically and economically. While new business types, such as coffee shops and the French restaurant, were starting to appear, family businesses opened by West Street indigenous residents were still in the majority.

Second wave of development: Geographical expansion and business investment

The more profound change came around the mid-2000s. In an effort to further develop its tourism economy, Yangshuo started a more comprehensive tourism development plan through economic-geographical expansion. In 2003, several connecting streets near West Street, including Xianqian Road, Binjiang Road, Guanlian Road, Chengzhong Road, Fuqian Lane and Guihua Road, also started to be developed (see Map 4.1). Existing old houses were renovated in accordance with the style of West Street so as to establish a 'big West Street', a concept proposed by the local government to expand the scope of the so-called 'global village' (Huang, 2009: 21–22). This project was further complemented by another investment worth tens of millions of Chinese yuan, making West Street a model tourism site of folk culture preservation

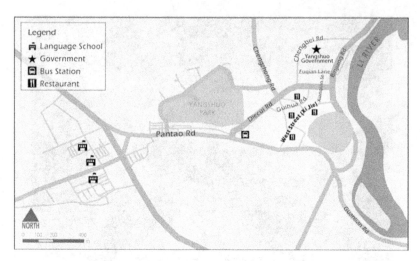

Map 4.1 West Street and its surroundings (impressionistic) (*Source:* Courtesy of Leonardo Zurita-Arthos).

(Chen, W. 2009: 359). Pointing to Guihua Road nearby, a local tour guide told me:

Extract 4.3

...this street used to be an old open-air grocery market. When the government invited bids for real estate development, the old grocery market was demolished. There were also residential houses, but they were actually too poor for people to live in. Nobody even dared to go to that street at night – it's dark and scary. But then houses were repaired and renovated so that they can now be used for businesses. (Field note, May 2011)

New businesses gradually appeared on these renovated streets. For example, Kelly's Café (see Figure 4.5) has been on Guihua Road for several years. It is quite popular among backpackers, and has even gained a recommendation from the backpackers' bible *Lonely Planet*. The café was opened by a local Chinese girl and it was rumored that she had been trained by a foreign chef. There were also some less famous but equally popular businesses. The Alley Bar (see Figure 4.6) was opened by an Austrian, and according to Philip, an English teacher from Canada, it was the best model of a traditional Western-style bar in Yangshuo, with beers from almost everywhere in the world – 'not drink just like Jack Daniel's, the stuff you can buy everywhere'.

Figure 4.5 Kelly's Café (*Source*: Photo by author, 2011)

Figure 4.6 The Alley Bar (*Source*: Photo by author, 2011)

However, while the nearby streets developed, West Street – the center of the so-called 'global village' and 'English Corner' – grew into an increasingly desirable piece of land for businesses, contributing to further investments for commercialization, mainly from middle-class businesspersons in Chinese cities. As Liu observes:

Extract 4.4

They [businesspersons] came and bid for the rental prices because they were trying to secure a place for their business. They used to pay rents like 700,000 yuan a year in big cities like Shanghai, so here they very willingly offered to pay us 200,000. They offered such good price themselves. But we'd never seen so much money before. So that's how now almost all the businesses are opened by non-locals.

According to him, the rental fees increased tenfold in a matter of two or three years after the severe acute respiratory syndrome (SARS) crisis (2002–2004). The houseowners on West Street also started to rent out their houses at a good price, and became the new-rich of the county, moving into much nicer and bigger houses elsewhere.[5] These incoming businesspersons arrived with profit-making plans and started to run more fancy establishments, in particular nightclubs and karaoke boxes, which changed the types of businesses on West Street. For example, near the west entrance of West Street, we still see 'Meiyou Café' (see Figure 4.7), but it has now changed hands (Wang, 2006a). While something similar to the old signboard is still there, another colorful neon signboard has been erected above it, which provides a service telephone number consisting

四楼休闲中心 (leisure centre on the fourth floor)

电话(Tel): 8882555

"没有" 会所 ('meiyou'club)

三楼豪华 KTV (luxury KTV on the third floor)

没有饭店 (Meiyou Café)

啤酒鱼 (beer fish)

Figure 4.7 Meiyou Café and others (*Source*: Photo by author, 2011)

of serial lucky numbers 8 and 5 (8882555), and announces in Chinese the availability of 'luxury KTV' (豪华KTV) on the third floor and a 'leisure centre' (休闲中心) on the fourth. On the first floor, we also see another restaurant, advertising the famous local dish 'beer fish' (啤酒鱼), which is claimed to have received coverage from the national television in China. In contrast to Kelly's Café (see Figure 4.5) and the Alley Bar (see Figure 4.6), and also very different from the former Meiyou Café (Figure 4.3), the new Meiyou Café now provides more extravagant services that could potentially attract big-spending Chinese tourists.

This, of course, is not the only business that has changed. As Harvey (1993) notes, a type of 'business coalition' always occurs as investors try to make the most of their businesses:

> those who have invested ... have to ensure that activities arise that render their investments profitable. Coalitions of entrepreneurs actively try to shape activities in places for this purpose... The 'social networking' which occurs in and through places to procure economic advantage may be intricate in the extreme but at the end of the day some sort of coalition, however shifting, is always in evidence. (Harvey, 1993: 6; see also Blommaert *et al.*, 2005: 221; Gotham, 2005: 1109)

West Street is now occupied by an increasing number of similar businesses that feature dancing and singing. Figure 4.8 shows another

Figure 4.8 男孩女孩 Boys & Girls Bar (*Source*: Photo by author, 2011)

Figure 4.9 西街零点酒吧 West Street Zero Point Bar (*Source*: Photo by author, 2011)

nightclub, which has a whole window wall facing the street with electronic signboards. More or less similar styles can also be seen along the street (see Figures 4.9 and 4.10). These bars usually have no English names, though the English word 'bar' does get on the signboard occasionally. Jason, an English teacher from South Africa who also played guitar at a quieter bar, told me,

Extract 4.5

West Street is more night clubs. People in China would call that bars, but I would call them night clubs, 'cause it's very loud music, everybody is dancing. Bar for me is somewhere you sit quietly and just talk.

These so-called bars tend to have dark halls or rooms lit only by dim neon lights. They usually open till the early morning hours, play loud and fast dance music and sometimes also feature pole dancers. According to Liu, they are the money-making machines on West Street:

Extract 4.6

…now if you still operate the business like before, putting out tables and let customers drink over beer and chat for hours, it definitely won't work,

Figure 4.10 四海爵色酒吧 Joys Bar (*Source*: Photo by author, 2011)

you get nothing! ... [with the rental fee so high] If you don't do clubs, it's very likely you will lose your money, because only selling expensive drinks brings profit. (Extracted from interview)

The existence of these 'bars' is quickly introducing new types of businesses and thus new ways of consumption and entertainment for tourists on what used to be a relatively traditional neighborhood street of souvenir shops and cafés. These businesses are not only redefining the use of space, but also prompting the appearance of other related, or what Harvey (1993: 6) calls somehow 'networked', businesses. Figure 4.11 shows several bars in a row. In-between there is one shop called 'Gobon' with a glaring white light, which sells sexual products (see Figure 4.12). Right next to Gobon is another souvenir shop. Here, we see three layers of signboards indicating the historical change of the former neighborhood. In the middle, there is a wooden signboard that says '民族饭店 nationality hotel'; above it, we see the glaring lights of a KTV; and below, 'Match Paradise'.[6] The lights on the four Chinese characters of 'nationality restaurant' are off, probably indicating that the former restaurant no longer exists and 'Match Paradise' seems to have taken over. Indeed, upon entering 'Match Paradise', I saw nothing resembling a restaurant, but a whole range of souvenir products with profane messages (see e.g. Figure 4.13).

Figure 4.11 Several bars in a row (*Source*: Photo by author, 2011)

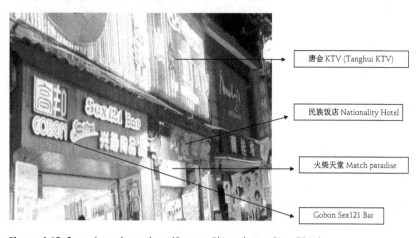

唐会 KTV (Tanghui KTV)

民族饭店 Nationality Hotel

火柴天堂 Match paradise

Gobon Sex121 Bar

Figure 4.12 Sexual products shop (*Source*: Photo by author, 2011)

Figure 4.13 'Beware the affaire!'

These shops contribute to what can be called an emerging nightclub culture and underground sex market. The following is an observation of West Street from a male's perspective:

Extract 4.7

Late in the afternoon, Cindy, my hotel owner, told me there were several people of similar age in the hall, and she asked whether I wanna go downstairs for a chat. I immediately seized this good opportunity to know tourists, and went down. And as I found out, one of them was a third year college student studying tourism in a college nearby. He also said he had been here a few times. So I started to talk to him a lot. 'Now West Street has become more commercialized', he told me. 'When I first came here, I did not expect here to be like this… Now the place is quite changed. When you go out, a pimp will ask you do you want a hooker? …When you go to West Street at night, you will see. They will just stop you, and ask "do you want a hooker?"'. (Field note, 12 May 2011)

As a female researcher, I was never approached in this way during my fieldwork, but I did notice some vulgar expressions on T-shirts that were put up by a T-shirt shop in a quite visible position along the street (Figure 4.14). It is not (necessarily) that people would wear them to find

Figure 4.14 Two T-shirts with traditional Chinese characters: left, 'Piaoke' (whore-master); right, 'Saohuo' (slut) (*Source*: Photo by author, 2011)

a hooker, but these calligraphic landscapes do point to the existence of a profane market.

In fact, the 'global village' keeps changing at a great rate. During the three months of my fieldwork, I witnessed several shops being renovated or changing hands, sometimes in a matter of several days, without me even noticing the process. A bar across the bridge near where I lived no longer had the same signboard when I noticed it again a few days later. I then remembered talking to the bar owner some time ago and he said he was heading to Guangdong to see whether there were opportunities there. I never saw him again. A little café, which used to be run by a Frenchman, had changed hands and was undergoing renovation into I don't know what. Also, I noticed a new souvenir shop opened on West Street, but I could not even recall what had been there before. So, what I have described so far only represents particular 'semiotic moments' (Stroud & Mpendukana, 2009: 363) in an ever-changing place.

Nevertheless, in this section, I have provided an outline of the demographic, spatial and semiotic change centered on West Street during the past three decades (see Table 4.1). These changes, as we have seen, involve the transformation of space by different layers of businesspersons. While the first wave of development started around a period of branding the traditional neighborhood already popular among international tourists to the domestic Chinese market, further developments

Table 4.1 Summary of historical change of West Street

Time	General sociogeographical change	General demographic, semiotic, material change
Till the late 1990s	Residential street with some family businesses	• Mainly residential houses, plus some small family businesses selling antiques, as well as a few cafés. • Opened by residents or people from nearby villages. • Rental fee (about 60 yuan per month in the mid-1980s).
First wave development (late 1990s to early 2000s)	Branding 'Global Village' and 'English Corner' (see also section 4.3 in Chapter 4)	• Inflows of businesspersons from elsewhere. • Increase in business types, for example, coffee shops. • Majority of the businesses are opened by local people. • Appropriation and commodification of English.
Second wave development (mid-2000s to 2011)	Geographical expansion and business investments	• Bifurcation of West Street and surrounding streets. • Relocation of West Street houseowners who have become the new-rich by renting houses out. • West Street: Inflow of business investors, increasing rental fee (200,000–300,000 yuan per year), increasing appearance of fancy nightclubs, few businesses by local Yangshuo people. • Surrounding streets: Rental fee cheaper than in West Street, mainly restaurants, cafés and relatively quieter bars, local foreigners' niche.

of the 'global village' since the mid-2000s have resulted in increasing inflows of private capital investment that have been redefining the social space demographically and semiotically. In the following sections, I look more closely at the current spatial organization of the 'global village' to see how we might understand the dialectic of signs, spatial practices and people (Blommaert, 2012: 59). In particular, how is the meaning of 'global village' being negotiated as a result of this second wave of mass commercialization? What does this change imply for the English language teaching business that constitutes an important part of the first wave of development?

Types of Space in the 'Global Village'

To provide a very broad picture, the following business types were observed on and around West Street in 2011:

- restaurants/cafés;
- coffee shops;
- bars/clubs;
- hotels;

- bakery/snack stores;
- clothes shops;
- souvenir shops;
- luggage stores;
- book/DVD stores;
- travel agencies.[7]

Generally speaking, the businesses run by Chinese people can at least manage to speak/write English, as well as different Chinese dialects, for the specific purpose of business transactions. And all the non-Chinese business owners I know[8] can speak English and at least survival Chinese. In all these businesses, it can be expected that English and Chinese are the main languages of communication, though due to the rather diverse sources of tourists and businesspersons, the language used can vary. Also, the language used in a business is not always the same as that of the business owner, or as indicated on the signboards. There is no simple correlation, because these businesses are not exclusive but open spaces to all potential tourists who care to go in, no matter where they are from and what languages they speak. These are what Blommaert *et al.* (2005: 215) call 'as-necessary dialogic places'.

Meng's coffee shop on West Street is one example. Meng comes from another city in Guangxi, and her shop uses a bilingual English–Chinese signboard. She opened her shop in 2003 with the help of a Taiwanese friend who had learned to make coffee and snacks in the United States back in the 1980s and 1990s. Her shop would start playing only Spanish music at around 11.00am every day. This is because as she got to know a Spanish-speaking Chinese tour guide for Spanish tourists, and as they became good friends, the tour guide would always bring Spanish tour groups to her coffee shop. This shop thus became the Spanish tourists' paradise. This despite the fact that Meng spoke no Spanish at all, and the waitress only managed to pick up some after serving many Spanish speakers. The tour guide would act as the translator, or the Spanish tourists would hopefully speak some English. Different groups of Spanish tourists would be brought to the coffee shop at the same time each day to enjoy the music as well as the coffee. Another example can be seen in the tourist messages in Tian's coffee shop (see Figure 4.15). Tian's shop (see Figure 4.16) has a Chinese language signboard, without an equivalent English name, though there is an English phrase 'the best coffee'. In the tourist messages, we see writings in Chinese, Japanese, Italian and Spanish, which testify to the diversity of the customers.[9]

[Chinese name omitted]
咖啡
(coffee)

The Best Coffee

Figure 4.15 A page from a customers' message book (*Source*: Photo by author, 2011)

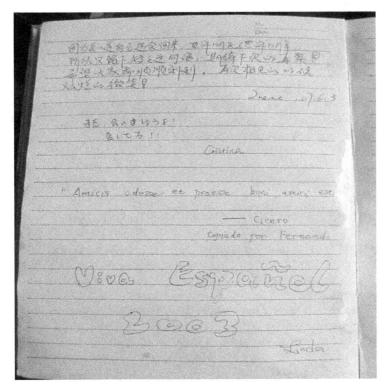

Figure 4.16 Tian's coffee shop (*Source*: Photo by author, 2011).

We see here the linguistic diversity in this 'global village' brought in by the constant and yet transient inflow of people from all over the world. While the former ethnolinguistic diversity is relatively local in its source and more stable in number and name, the new linguistic diversity generated by the tourism industry is more global in origin, transient in time and unpredictable in number and name.[10] The specific language used is also contingent on the particular tasks at hand, on the interlocutors one has and on the specific place one is in. This constant inflow and outflow of people indicates that West Street is a very open space for speakers of different languages. This is also the image depicted for West Street in the media, a truly global place where people and goods from around the world mix and match and live together in peace (see Chapter 3).

Then, how to make sense of a 'global village' that seems to be open to everyone? How to provide a critical assessment of the image of free flows, as represented by the media? To address these issues, we need to step back from language for a while and turn to spatial function, an insight from Dell Hymes as cited in Blommaert (2010):

> ... it will not do to begin with language, or a standard linguistic description, and look outward to social context. A crucial characteristic of the sociolinguistic approach is that it looks in toward language, as it were, from its social matrix. To begin with language, or with an individual code, is to invite the limitations of a purely correlational approach, and to miss much of the organization of linguistic phenomena. (Hymes, 1974: 75, as cited in Blommaert, 2010: 10–11)

To achieve a more differentiated understanding of the flows in and around West Street, it is important to distinguish several different ways in which tourist spaces may be used. Although the businesses I have referred to are potentially open to all tourists/customers, different businesses also cater to people with different patterns of consumption and mobility. Hotels are for people on the road – they are *spaces of privacy* that are supposed to offer people rest and peace of mind in a relatively busy and strange tourist destination. Bakery/snack stores, clothes shops, souvenir shops, book stores and luggage stores, as well as vendor stalls, are *spaces of transaction* where customers are supposed to simply come, buy (or not buy) their items and leave. Restaurants/cafés, coffee shops and bars/clubs, on the other hand, are *spaces of sociability* where people do not simply buy food and drink but are likely to consume them in the environment provided. In fact, as we all know, the physical, social and semiotic ambience can be a very important consideration in customers' choice.

Admittedly, what I have outlined above is only intended to be true from a *touristic business perspective*, and represents a very rough categorization. As Blommaert *et al.* (2005: 207) make clear, space is multifunctional and susceptible to 'the kind of intervention that is oriented to a *redefinition* of the space' (Blommaert *et al.*, 2005: 219, italics original). For example, one can imagine that a business house might be a place for the business owner to sleep after midnight, therefore making it a space not of transaction but of privacy. Also, friends of a souvenir store owner might go to him/her for whatever reason and they might start chitchatting over tea. In this way, the owner can be 'disturbed', so to speak, by also having to serve customers when they arrive. Or for me, there were some 'disturbing' moments when the business owner had to go to serve customers in the middle of our interview. Nevertheless, a rough typology of touristic uses of space provides a useful starting point for more nuanced analysis.

So, focusing on spaces of sociability in particular, restaurants/cafés, coffee shops and bars/clubs tend to be spaces where people travelling or living around Yangshuo can hang out. Generally, people entering these spaces would expect to socialize, as opposed to retreat into their private life or make a brief transaction. For long-term staying tourists, in particular, they would most probably socialize with each other and form social networks here. Second, there are also varied *styles of sociability*. We have seen that bars on West Street and its surrounding streets are, generally speaking, different spaces semiotically, which provide different physical environments and aesthetic experiences. The differentiation of space arising from tourism investment may also mean that former spatial orders are disturbed, and that the new spatial order might have to exist in tension with the former ones. Here, we might see interspatial dynamics, that is, how businesses co-exist as spaces of different types and styles. I will elaborate on these nuances in the next section.

Contentious Lives in the 'Global Village'

Closing down and moving away

As we have seen, the second wave of tourism investment has brought in new businesses on West Street, many of which are nightclubs. These businesses have introduced new styles of sociability but have also created interspatial tensions with older businesses established during the 1990s and early 2000s. In this subsection, I focus on how types of space, styles of sociability and styles of living emerge as sources of tension among business owners in this changing 'global village'. I show this through one case of closing down and three cases of moving away.

Figure 4.17 Protest placard by Henry's hotel. (*Source*: Photo by author, 2011)[11]

In Chapter 2, I introduced a protest placard at Henry's hotel, which is reproduced here for convenience (Figure 4.17). As already indicated, this is not to be considered merely as an incidental case but points toward the tensions around the spatial transformation of West Street in general. Let me very briefly reproduce the story here before attempting further explanations.

This sign was placed at the entrance to Henry's already closed hotel – it was no longer accepting customers though still 'welcomes anyone interested to come in and have a look', as stated in the text. The reason for the closure was given to be the ongoing construction of a nightclub next door (see Figure 4.18), which had been (and would be) interfering with what was supposed to be a quiet, cozy hotel. This issue was raised with the local bureau of construction but failed to receive any due attention from the officials who, according to the owner, were indifferent. Hence the placard shown in Figure 4.17.

Figure 4.18 'Construction is in progress' (*Source*: Photo by author, 2011)

The hotel had been running in a relatively congenial business environment for about 10 years. Actually, the hotel already had a nightclub next door that had been a little disturbing to it, but now the construction of a second nightclub on the other side would make the hotel inoperable. When Henry first came to Yangshuo in 1998 from the United States and opened his hotel in 2002, it was because he liked the beautiful natural scenery and the nice little neighborhood. But now everything had changed, worse than he could ever imagine:

Extract 4.8

It's changed too much. It's too bad. This is very disappointing ...because it used to be a very special street, and very unique atmosphere draws people here. But now it's just a noisy place, you know. There's about 16 bars and discos, a lot of noise and music. It's hard to talk to people, it's too noisy. And it's not a good location for a hotel any more. ...

The discos make a lot of money every year. That's the best business on West Street. But if people like to drink, get drunk, and hear loud music, watch naked girls pole-dancing, that's what they are doing.

What we see here is a tension in the use of space between a hotel owner and a nightclub owner. A nightclub, as a space of sociability featuring loud music and dancing crowds, is located next to a hotel, a space of privacy that is meant to provide a peaceful haven for its customers.

The interspatial dynamics are also shown through people moving out. While Henry was trying hard to protest on West Street, some businesspeople had already relocated to much quieter streets with affordable houses nearby. While the increasing rental fee counted as a major concern, moving out was also a way to regain the quiet and casual atmosphere that had been the original reason for living in Yangshuo. When it first opened in 2000, Tian's coffee shop was located on West Street, but it moved to Binjiang Road in 2009 after the rent increased. The shop now has a very nice view of the Li River and the mountains across the river. Tian explained why they decided to move:

Extract 4.9

West Street started to change around 2004 or 2006. A house of only about 30 or 40m^2 would cost several hundreds of thousands [a year]. We are here just for a lifestyle. If things become too expensive, it no longer makes sense for us. ...Like many others, we arrived here for a simple life, and opened the business just to make a living. But with the rental fees so high, there would be too much pressure. We could make money there, but that's not the life we want. ...West Street has become too noisy. There are always drunk people on the street, they are not the customers we want.

Moving out to regain a more peaceful and less competitive life is also what Song and her Singaporean husband had decided to do in 2007. She started off on West Street in 1995, and was now on Guihua Road:

Extract 4.10

Those with Karaoke's make big money. For us little restaurants, even if we want to make 200 or 300 a day, we would have to work our ass off. ... We were on West Street first in 1995, making coffees and dishes. But what can we do now? West Street has become too expensive, 2 or 3 hundreds of thousands [a year]. It is very difficult [for us]. Everybody wants to outdo everybody. We hope to still have some relaxation, without too much pressure.

Making coffee, preparing dishes and just living a simple life, these life-styles are no longer sustainable on West Street.

Similar laments are also voiced by Sun. 'West Street used to be like, we would put tables along the streets, tourists would sit there, have their beers, and we chat about whatever they see or do during their travelling in the day. That kind of life, it's such a memory and I miss it a lot'. In his late fifties, Sun is respectfully called a 'master' by the locals. He is keen on traditional Chinese culture and could be seen as a living symbol of it: he wears traditional loose Chinese shirts and pants and keeps a Taoist hair knot or sometimes just wears his hair loose. He is also famous for his artistic practices in painting, calligraphy and Chinese seal carving. He used to be a farmer in another village in Yangshuo, before moving to West Street to do some carving in 1985; he opened his café there in 1992 until 2003. He is cheerful and talkative, as everyone can tell, and has made friends with many tourists – he learned English by himself – who still visit him in his new place these days when they return.

He is disappointed by the change of West Street – he said it's become a Wenzhou village, which means everything is about money now, as Wenzhou is a city famous in China for its many rich entrepreneurs with private enterprises. He has now left his former little café on West Street, and has opened a new one next to the little hotel I stayed in. Obviously, he could not make much money from it. Few tourists would find their way to this relatively quiet place and on several visits I saw that his restaurant was closed. He said he would rather sacrifice money for the sake of a way of life he prefers: 'people there are gold-diggers. I don't want to go there, haven't been there for some time. Here, I have my quietness. As to whether I can have customers, I don't care'. As we talked, he very happily went in to fetch a seal he had just finished carving. 'This is a very high quality stone, a gift from a friend', he said while proudly showing it to me. Inside his restaurant, his calligraphy writings decorate the walls. He now lives at the Xu Beihong Residence, which is located on the same street as his restaurant, where he works as a housekeeper. He takes care of the residence and spends time painting and writing calligraphy almost every day. While lamenting that West Street has become a Wenzhou village, he also shared with me his dream image of West Street. He said it should be like 'Along the River During the Qingming Festival', a renowned Song Dynasty painting of a city where people enjoy their lives together in a harmonious and laid-back atmosphere (summary of unrecorded conversation, 30 June 2011).

So far, we have seen four cases of interspatial tensions among older and new West Street businesses. The business owners, Chinese and foreign, who arrived during the first wave of tourism development, are now coping with the sociogeographical change of West Street in varied ways. All of them started off opening up businesses on West Street with the desire to live in a nice physical environment. Their lifestyles, according to their accounts, were also closely interconnected with the spaces of sociability they provided for tourists. Note that Sun had enjoyed having many tourist friends through the years of running his café, and Tian was concerned that on West Street the potential customers, who tend to be drunk, were not people he would like to see in his coffee shop. Song also said that she did not enjoy living in a street where 'everyone wants to outdo everyone'. And Henry's protest was actually not just about that one nightclub under construction. He mentioned how West Street had changed so much that when 'there's about 16 bars and discos, a lot of noise and music. ...it's not a good location for a hotel any more'. Their cases show how in the second wave of tourism development, early business owners had to adjust themselves in varied ways to a fast-changing place as they found themselves no longer compatible with West Street as a space of consumption and entertainment. While perhaps not in the extreme sense, these people might be considered victims of the dispossessing power of neoliberal space (Peck & Tickell, 2002: 389) or of what Massey (1993) calls 'the power-geometry of space', or also cases of what Blommaert (2010: 154) calls 'soft marginalization', that is 'the marginalization of particular cultural features, identities, practices'. In the next subsection, we will see that there are further complications.

Local foreigners' niche of sociability in Yangshuo

One unplanned consequence of the geographical expansion of and tourism investment in West Street, as we have already seen, is that the relatively quieter streets now tend to be occupied by businesspersons with less economic capital who run relatively modest businesses, as opposed to expensive West Street clubs. As Harvey (1993: 6) observes, 'to say... that place construction is a given in the logic of capitalism's production of space is not to argue that the geographical pattern is determined in advance'. Businesses on quieter streets, especially those that moved from West Street, have helped keep the 'traditional' ambience of West Street to some extent. As Yan told me, 'this [Guihua road] is what West Street used to be like ten years ago'. In this subsection, I look at how some businesses on these quieter streets have become the local foreigners' niche of sociability, and how their niche of sociability is nevertheless fraught with the issue of multifunctionality of space (Blommaert et al., 2005: 207) due to English educational tourism.

It is estimated that there are about 200 foreigners working at local language schools in Yangshuo (He, 2011: 56–57), and their relatively long-term stay has gained them the name of 'local foreigners'. They teach at school, get to know people and socialize in Yangshuo while touring around (see Chapter 5 for details). Jason was an English teacher from South Africa. He was also a guitar player in Ding's Bar on Guihua Road, where he played with his band members who were from different parts of the world:

Extract 4.11

Well, kind of, I talk to people, meet everybody, I just make friends, and then know, oh okay you play this or that. So I got introduced to a local Chinese guy. He's a drummer from Guilin, and he moves here and we're already friends, and we just meet each other at the bar. And he said do you wanna play music, we play music together? Just me and him. And then, yeah, we kind of decided we're always looking for more people. If there's another guy can play, then we just speak, and get contact, and it's quite easy if you find the right people, it works easily you know. … We now have another guitar player from California, America, the piano player from Switzerland, and we will have a new singer, from Australia.

The bar Jason played in was also very popular among foreigners. Talking about bars in Yangshuo in general, Jason said:

Extract 4.12

Every bar has its place in Yangshuo, I think. Like we might go out and started at Alley bar, and sit there and relax, and you drink more and maybe decide okay let's go dance a little bit, so you might end up at a bar with club, with dancing, for instance.

He then noted further that for Westerners in general they have preferences about which bars to frequent:

Extract 4.13

West Street bars are, … I mean, I've been there a few time, but er I think westerners feel more relaxed more at home around more western faces, around western people. …so westerners like more relaxed bars, …But I think everyone has different taste in music, in their choice, their party. Things like I guess a lot of western tourists come here are what you would call backpackers, okay? And they're more relaxed people, and they prefer the relax bars, so that they can talk to each other and got to know people.

A similar preference was also noted by Steve, an English teacher from Ireland. He had been staying in Yangshuo for a few months, teaching part-time at different schools while travelling around. Because he enjoyed Yangshuo, he planned to renew his Chinese visa later in Hong Kong. Like other teachers, he had found his 'niche' in Yangshuo, and socialized a lot on Guihua Road. That day, we were doing the interview at a restaurant of his choice on Guihua Road. 'Most of the tourism things seem to be concentrated on West Street, which is good I guess', he said, 'because we can sit here now, and it's not extremely busy'. In the following extract, he talked about why he liked Guihua Road by way of contrast with West Street:

Extract 4.14

Steve: I think it [West Street]'s trying to emulate some sort of night clubs in the west, maybe. That's what West Street [is], I guess. Maybe they think this is what western people like. So yeah, they got these bars, and extremely loud terrible music, and very loud like dance music, with pole-dancers, expensive drinks. Yeah, you find most westerners in Yangshuo don't go to these places, as we are not interested ...Honestly, I'm not a fan of West Street.

Shuang: Okay.

Steve: Yeah, I think er they er. But I can understand that the local people they want to make as much money as possible. So they know that, they understand that tourists would go there. Yeah. Sure, it always going to be as busy as it is. But, yeah, I don't know, it's extremely touristic and noisy. ...This is the same in every country. When you first go to a city, you go to where the guidebook tells you to go, or where it's popular, so you go to West Street. And then you'll discover, okay, this is like everywhere, this is like Khaosan road in Bangkok, or Temple Bar in Dublin. It's where the expensive, noisy bars are all there, souvenir shops are, well, you know. I don't know, it's, it's terrible... I don't know. People just go because it's convenient. And they don't know any better. If you are willing to look around, there are so much, so much better place at Yangshuo. I most prefer here [Guihua road]. And I prefer the older parts of Yangshuo, with traditional bars. I would most like to have a drink there. Even in my own city, I don't understand why the music has to be so loud. There's a term we would use to describe it, tourist trap, yeah tourist trap. In

Figure 4.19 McDonald's at the west end of West Street (*Source*: Photo by author, 2011)

many parts of the world, they have beautiful places, but they use it too much, with many bars, restaurants, McDonald's, KFC's. I can understand they're trying to make money, but you may end up destroying what makes it unique in the first place.... The first thing I thought on West Street is how out of place McDonald's was [see Figure 4.19].

Shuang: Out of place?

Steve: Yeah.

Shuang: What do you mean?

Steve: Out of place means it should not be here.

Shuang: Why, why it should not be here?

Steve: Because you have so many beautiful mountains here, things you have never seen. And you have things in the way of the beautiful view. It's giant yellow M, with... It's pretty disgraceful. I don't know why they were allowed to do this, because the thing about Yangshuo is no matter where you are, you are got to see a beautiful view. So you shouldn't put terrible things, like a giant yellow M from McDonald's to block these views.
...

Here, we see that the formation of a local foreigners' niche in Yangshuo is driven by the increasingly touristic and commercialized West Street on the one hand, and also by race- and culture-based differences in taste ('everyone has different taste in music, in their choice, their party', 'westerners feel more relaxed more at home around more western faces, around western people', 'you find most westerners in Yangshuo don't go to these places, as we are not interested'). For instance, while Jason plays in the band with a Chinese drummer friend and may hang out in many different spaces of sociability ('Every bar has its place in Yangshuo', 'West Street bars are, ... I mean, I've been there a few time, but...'), this is actually an alternative to the preferred way of socializing 'around western faces' feeling 'more relaxed more at home'. This indicates that in this transnational space there is some sort of division along race (c.f. Amin, 2013: 4; Valentine, 2008: 330, 334).

But, as foreigners find their niche of sociability, it also in some way provides a means for people who would like to practice spoken English with foreigners, in particular the English language students in local language schools, as we shall see in Chapter 5. While as an English teacher, Jason knows that students, including his own, tend to approach him to practice their English, he sometime still has to deal with unexpected situations when people approach him for free English lessons. He recalled once a student who came up to him holding a dictionary after one of his guitar performances. He loves interacting with different people, he said, but 'this is too much'.

Sometimes, the use of bars for English learning opportunities not only exists as a side-function, but tends to become a dominant one if the number of students increases. The students, as we shall see in Chapter 5, tend to be lower-middle-class professionals coming to learn English after quitting their jobs, so they tend to be careful with their money. According to Philip, who often went to hang out with Jason, 'students would often sit together and occupy a large table. But they only order one beer, and share among themselves. This is not good for the business, you know' (Field note, 9 July 2011). Because of this, measures sometimes have to be taken to deter the improper use of space, as Kay told me:

Extract 4.15

Kay: There's one bar particular, it's called [name of bar] and I, I know that at one stage, I don't know, at one stage, she's charging Chinese people 50 yuan just to go to the bar.

Shuang: Really?

Kay: Because there were so many students that were trying to speak with the foreigners. And the foreigners were getting irritated. And the foreigners were starting to not go. It's a favorite, many foreigners like going there. And because of that many student went. And yes, she had to do something, to almost to keep the students away.

Shuang: Okay.

Kay: Em. But basically any bar that gets many foreigners and is not too noisy tends to be popular. The longer you're here, it irritates you more and more.

Here, we see that the quieter streets surrounding West Street have generally kept a more relaxed ambience. This attracts local foreigners who prefer to relax and socialize in traditional, quieter bars, as opposed to fancy, noisy ones. However, the local foreigners' niche of sociability is at the same time being used by students who come to look for English conversations. This indicates a complexity in the use of space in that these businesses provide spaces for particular styles of sociability that are favored by foreigners, who in turn are people with valuable linguistic resources for language learners, whose arrival, nevertheless, also introduces a new and conflicting functionality to these businesses as spaces for practicing spoken English. Therefore, complicating the concern of the local official mentioned in the introduction, the tensions and developmental dilemma of the so-called 'global village' derive not just from the different preferences of different customers. The expansion and commercial development of West Street, as we have seen, results in cases of closing down and moving out, which account for part of the tensions around space due to mass commercialization. To further complicate the picture, it is the commodification of English through educational tourism that leads to the unexpected multifunctionality (Blommaert *et al.*, 2005) of the local foreigners' niche. In other words, the tensions around space do not just lie in the commercial development of West Street; language and communication can also be important sources of tensions around the control over, access to and functionality of space.

Summary

This chapter aims to understand the local dynamics of the so-called 'global village'. I have drawn on mixed evidence to (1) outline the historical processes of the sociogeographical change of West Street during the past three decades, and (2) provide a glimpse of the current local dynamics arising from this historical change. I have shown that three phases of change can be observed in the recent history of West Street, with the most comprehensive change occurring since the mid-2000s through geographical expansion and tourism business investment. In this process, the demographic and semiotic change results in differentiation of spatial organization. To explore potential tensions, I proposed that West Street might be examined through a typology of *spaces of privacy*, *spaces of transaction* and *spaces of sociability*. I also noted that there are complications due to different styles of sociability, potential interspatial dynamics, as well as multifunctionality of space (Blommaert *et al.*, 2005). By examining two groups of people living in this 'global village', business owners and local foreigners, I demonstrated how the branding and business investment in West Street have brought about tensions to each group as they live and adjust themselves in different, but related, ways. On the one hand, commercial investment in West Street has led to the relocation of some businesses into quieter streets nearby. On the other, as quieter streets become local foreigners' niches, they are also subject to the redefinition of space by Chinese people who want to practice English.

Therefore, complicating the convivial image of intercultural encounters depicted in the tourism promotional discourses, we see that there are tensions around space. And the tensions involve more than just the preferences of different customers, but also point toward the reorganization and use of space as mediated by mass commercialization and commodification of English. Through tracing the multiple mobilities of people in the historical transformation of space, and delineating the geographical trajectories of business owners and local foreigners, we see how semiotic, spatial and aesthetic differences are lived out through the multiple ways that people carry on their daily lives in this global village. Hannam *et al.* (2006: 4, italics original) observe that, 'in their search for spatial *ordering*, the social sciences have still failed to fully recognize how the spatialities of social life presuppose, and frequently involve conflict over, both the actual and the imagined movements of people from place to place, event to event' (see also Amin, 2013; Valentine, 2008). While the 'global village' might not be a site of conflict in the extreme sense wherein people are seriously displaced, I hope I have shown in this chapter that by examining the varied ways that people talk about, move around and live in the space they inhabit, we start to see at least the power of space that may result in exclusion and marginalization. Language and communication, in particular, constitute important bases for exploring these issues. We already have a glimpse of the tensions around the multifunctionality of space due to the commodification of English; in the next chapter, I turn to the interactional practice of talking to foreigners per se and explore in detail how exactly language learning proceeds in the 'global village'.

Notes

(1) This is the only statistical data I can find regarding language use in Yangshuo.

(2) This is my literal translation of the name of the dialect. I was unable to find the official English equivalent.

(3) The Zhuang language belongs to the Zhuang-Dong (also called Kam-Tai) languages of the Tai-Kadai language family (Bodomo, 2010: 180). Its many varieties, due to the uneven geographic distribution of the Zhuang people, are sometimes categorized into Northern Zhuang and Southern Zhuang by dialectologists (Edmondson, 1994). There are two different writing systems for the Zhuang language, one based on the Chinese character writing system, the other on Latin alphabets (Bodomo, 2010: 181). The latter enjoys an official status, codified on the basis of a northern variety Wuming Zhuang dialect in 1957 (*Nanning Evening Paper*, 2013).

(4) Writing spring couplets (春联 chūn lián) on red paper and posting them on both sides and the top of doors is a traditional Chinese New Year practice. The couplets typically express good wishes and aspirations for the new year.

(5) I was unable to find and talk to an indigenous West Street houseowner. But one local Yangshuo resident in her mid-twenties told me, 'The indigenous West Street residents are rich now, and would call themselves West Street people, instead of Yangshuo people. They rent their houses out and make big money every year. They do not even have to work anymore. They live in nice villas and send their kids abroad to study. They just think they're different ... West Street is a walking street, and there should be no cars, but some former West Street residents are just being rude by driving directly to their own houses on West Street. You know, there's a tradition here that people should not die at hospitals but at their own houses so that the prosperity of the family could carry on for generations. I once saw a car driving directly into West Street, causing a stir in the crowd. Then several people got off, carrying an old lady almost green in color. I was so terrified and stood stiff there. They carried the old lady upstairs to their old house so that she could die there to let the family's fortune continue' (Field note, 1 July 2011).

(6) 'Match' here means lighting matches, as indicated by the Chinese name.

(7) In Yangshuo, some business houses tend to provide multiple types of business services, though the main business remains the one as advocated on the signboard. Inside some restaurants and coffee shops, for example, there are books and magazines on display, both for browsing inside and for sale (see Appendix B). Hotels in Yangshuo also provide touring services through cooperation with tour guides and travel agencies. The little hotel I stayed in provides touring brochures for tourists, arranges tours for individual travelers upon request, rents bicycles and even sells tickets for shows and performances. The night keeper of the hotel used to be a tour guide in another province in China, and he told me that in his hometown, hotels are forbidden from providing touristic and guiding services, but in Yangshuo this is allowed and prevalent (Field note, 1 June 2011).

(8) I know five foreign business owners, including Kay (South African), Henry (American), Philip (Canadian, who works as a teacher but also runs a hotel), Cindy (Malaysian) and Song's husband (Singaporean). According to Philip, the owner of the Alley Bar (Austrian) can also speak Chinese.

(9) Certainly, there are valid reasons to question whether we can tell the writer's nationality or ethnicity from the written languages alone, and unfortunately I have little ethnographic evidence to argue this. Indeed, based on my rough examination of more than 200 pages of customers' messages in the shop, the code itself may not necessarily tell where the writer is from. In one instance, a person wrote in not so fluent Chinese characters, but in her signage she wrote that she was an American living in the city of Changsha, China (see Appendix C). Nevertheless, I did observe handwritten languages as diverse as English, French, Spanish, Japanese, Korean, Italian, as well as Chinese (in either simplified or traditional characters), which presumably shows the diversity of customers.

(10) See Appendix E for statistics on tourism in Yangshuo from 2000 to 2010. No data on the 'global village' alone are available. Nevertheless, since the 'global village' constitutes an important site for the entire Yangshuo tourism system, these numbers could provide a rough sense of tourism in the 'global village'. Statistics were obtained from the statistics office of the Yangshuo Tourism Bureau during fieldwork in 2011.

(11) One might be observant enough to notice that the traditional orthography of Chinese is used here. It is actually a common practice to use the traditional instead of the simplified orthography in calligraphic writings, among the older generation in particular, and in other artistic writings. See Appendix D for the carving of 'Yangshuo' as '陽朔' instead of '阳朔' along the river dock. According to Qin (2004), the two characters '陽朔' were first written by the then vice-president of Guangxi, Huang Yun, and then carved onto the stone by two professionals in 1982. There were three considerations in the carving: first, to inform people of the place name; second, decorative; third, it is also a cultural landscape (Qin, 2004: 329).

5 Global Village as 'English Corner': 'Enjoy Speaking English All the Time'

As we already know, Yangshuo provides opportunities for people to improve their spoken English by interacting with foreigners, in particular through what is known as 'English Educational Tourism' (xiūxué yóu 修学游). The following is an extract from the website of Samuel Language School, provided in a Q&A session as a reply to 'Who is this school for?':

Extract 5.1

Harry, with a bachelor's degree, obtained his Band-6 certificate[1] in English during his college years. He worked as a financial manager in a company in Shenzhen … After seeing our school on the internet, he immediately added our website to his Favorites toolbar, and asked for a leave of one month to study here. But he felt that he had not enjoyed himself enough here for staying just one month, so he simply quitted his high-salary job and studied for another two months.

When people who did not understand asked why he quitted such a good job, he explained like this: 1. You have all the chances in the world to make money, but there are not many chances like having a good time studying here. You cannot only improve your English, but also relax among the nice scenery of rivers and mountains. 2. The expenditure for learning three months here is even less than learning for just one month in Guangzhou, Shenzhen, or Zhuhai. The price is so good. 3. The learning environment here is unique, and cannot be found in other places in China. Every night you can chat with foreigners over beer. Where else can you find such feelings?

As we shall see, actual language learning in Yangshuo is not as glorious as this sketch might suggest; however, the large number of foreigners and relatively low cost of learning have made Yangshuo an attractive and affordable place among lower-middle-class working professionals seeking to improve

Figure 5.1 'Yangshuo: The first bilingual town in China' (*Source*: Photo by author, 2011)

their English. Since the initial development of educational tourism in the late 1990s, Yangshuo now claims to be 'the biggest English Corner in China' (Yangshuo Tourism Bureau, 2009). Around the areas where several language schools are located, slogans are painted along the walls, declaring the town a bilingual town (see Figure 5.1) and a place to 'enjoy

Figure 5.2 'Enjoy speaking English all the time' (*Source*: Photo by author, 2011)

speaking English all the time' (see Figure 5.2). It is estimated that there are about 30 language schools staffed by more than 200 foreign language teachers, and each year Yangshuo in total attracts an average of more than 6000 people, coming to learn English since 2003 (He, 2011: 56–57).

In this chapter, I examine the language learning industry in Yangshuo; however, before doing so, it is worth looking at similar language learning establishments elsewhere.

The Political Economy of 'English Corner'

It is well established that English language learning is increasingly characterized by varied mobilities of people, materials and semiotic resources, and these mobilities are closely linked with imaginations of space and place (Gao & Park, 2015; Park & Bae, 2009: 366–367). On the one hand, language learners adopt transnational migration as one of their educational strategies as they seek to improve their English in English-speaking countries (e.g. Kobayashi, 2011; Park & Bae, 2009). On the other hand, programs aiming to provide equally attractive language learning experiences, but without students having to pass immigration borders, have also been set up through what are variously known as 'English villages/towns' or 'foreign language theme parks' in South Korea (see Park, 2009) and Japan (see Seargeant, 2005). These English villages import infrastructural materials from the West and hire staff from native English-speaking countries to provide students with an 'authentic' learning environment that boasts 'more English than England itself' (Seargeant, 2005: 327).

Despite the popularity of English villages, they have generated debates about pedagogical effectiveness (see Krashen, 2006; Trottier, 2008), as well as language ideologies underpinning such educational establishments (Seargeant, 2005). Seargeant (2005: 332) observes that with the ever-increasing numbers of non-native English speakers, there is a shift in conceptualizing authenticity as no longer residing in interaction with native speakers but with 'effective communication via English as a lingua franca'. Examining the case of British Hills, where native English speakers are employed to work in a simulated Western environment through role play, providing school-age children with an 'authentic' experience of living in the West and interacting with native speakers, Seargeant (2005: 341–342) argues that the English village contradicts a neutral model of English as an international lingua franca by reproducing an ideology of nativeness.

While these studies consider the issues of pedagogical justification (e.g. Krashen, 2006; Trottier, 2008) and the politics of authentic English (e.g. Seargeant, 2005), in this chapter I hope to demonstrate that we can also ask different questions from different analytical perspectives. Focusing on the way that Chinese working professionals practice English with foreigners in Yangshuo, my purpose is not to evaluate the effectiveness of this learning method, nor do I seek to find out whether learning English eventually helps them achieve their professional goals. Rather, I focus on how English language learning is defined here, and how language learning proceeds. Specifically, I examine the observed phenomenon of practicing English with foreigners in Yangshuo as an 'activity type', that is, a 'recognized activity... whose local members are goal-defined, socially constituted, bounded' (Levinson, 1979: 368), in particular with regard to how such learning activity is embedded in the changing political economy of China.

In pursuing lines of inquiry beyond the concerns of previous studies, I am aligning with what Rampton (1997a) characterizes as a retuning of applied linguistics toward the socially constituted linguistics that Hymes (1977) identified decades ago (Rampton, 1997a: 8; see also Rampton, 1995, 1997b, 1997c, 2006). Such retuning requires 'tak[ing] on larger political, social or educational ideas and try[ing] to work through what they mean in linguistic and discursive detail' (Rampton, 1997a: 10). This perspective, as we will see, contributes much to our understanding of the case of Yangshuo.

First, tourism can be understood as a mechanism of mobility that drives the movement of semiotic, material and educational resources, while concurrently redefining their meanings. While English villages in Japan have been characterized as 'purpose-built enclaves' that 'symbolically position English outside the boundary of mainstream society' (Seargeant, 2005: 342), the case of Yangshuo conforms more to what Sheller and Urry (2006: 214) call 'places of movement': 'places are dynamic, they are about proximities, about the bodily co-presence of people who happen to be in that place at that time, doing activities together'. As I will show, the English Corner in Yangshuo exists in a parasitic relationship with an existing tourism community. In other words, it is already a place of constant flows that are then strategically managed for English language learning.

Second, the management of varied mobilities for language education constitutes an important part of the strategic development of the local economy. This interconnectivity of tourism and education has already been documented in the field of tourism management. Cooper and Latham (1988: 331), for example, observed that the UK government had been actively encouraging educational visits, and they noted that 'there are sound economic reasons for attracting educational groups as they often … provide a much needed contribution to fixed costs at a time when there may otherwise be few visitors'. I will show specific ways in which local entrepreneurs and the local government steer this language learning industry in Yangshuo by means of managing tourist mobilities as part of the local tourism economy.

Following on from this, people brought together under this management of flows engage in expected and unexpected interactions. To examine how these communicative complexities are lived out, we cannot safely assume what will or could occur in these social occasions. We can only know through ethnographic analysis. As far as I know, little has been documented about how exactly learning proceeds in English villages. By examining the observed phenomenon of practicing English with foreigners in Yangshuo as an 'activity type' (Levinson, 1979: 368), I will explore how such learning activity is embedded in the changing political economy of China, thereby contributing to the emerging research on the intersection of language and neoliberalism (Gray, 2010; Holborow, 2015; Park, 2010a, 2013; Piller & Cho, 2013; Price, 2014).

Neoliberalism can be understood as a shifting relationship between market and state wherein the market is acclaimed as the best guidance for economic practice, and the unleashing of individual freedom and entrepreneurship in a free market the best way to achieve personal welfare (Harvey, 2005: 2). Neoliberalism, therefore, is not just an economic theory, but a hegemonic discourse that affects people's everyday conduct, such that individuals' entrepreneurial virtues, as opposed to systematic structures, are to be held accountable for personal success or failure (Harvey, 2005: 65–65). In other words, neoliberalism can be seen as the hegemonic transformation of subjectivity (Read, 2009: 26). This understanding of neoliberalism, or what (Ong, 2007: 4) calls 'neoliberalism with a small "n"', moves beyond neoliberalism as just an economic doctrine or market ideology, and examines it as 'a technology of governing'. Under a neoliberal regime, the ideal figure of the neoliberal self is supposed to take initiatives, make calculated choices and use entrepreneurship in the cultivation of self as 'self-actualizing or self-enterprising subjects' (Ong, 2007: 5; Urciuoli, 2008; Yan, 2003), destabilizing the old politics of self based on communitarian solidarity and common good (Read, 2009). As Thatcher most famously put it, 'there is no such thing as society, only individual men and women… economics are the method, but the object is to change the soul' (as quoted in Harvey, 2005: 23). Such conception of self has now become a new regime of truth, but its hegemony is achieved not through censorship but through unleashing personal desires, freedom and entrepreneurship. This conforms to what Foucault (1991) calls governmentality wherein the government of self gets internalized as a moral issue instead of passive obedience to external violence or coercion. As Ong (2006: 4) elaborates: 'following Foucault, "governmentality" … covers a range of practices that "constitute, define, organize and instrumentalize the strategies that individuals in their freedom can use in dealing with each other". Neoliberal governmentality results from the infiltration of market-driven truths and calculations. … individuals…are then induced to self-management according to market principles of discipline, efficiency, and competitiveness'.

However, the ideal figure of the neoliberal self is not reproduced seamlessly in everyday life without tensions. While some people, as Harvey (2005) reminds us, social elites in particular, are more apt at and therefore benefit from such new rules of the neoliberal economy, other people may struggle with it or simply never catch up (Piller & Cho, 2013). The triumphant dominance of neoliberalism on the global scale partly depends on its rhetoric of resorting to social and moral values of wide appeal, e.g. freedom, while disguising its goals of wealth accumulation and the restoration or creation of elite power (Harvey, 2005). Such disjuncture is arguably the 'most essential feature' of neoliberalism (Brenner & Theodore, 2002: 353). In reality, neoliberalism has created the most unequal world in recent human history (George, 1999; Harvey, 2005), and is differently experienced by different social groups and individuals (Ong, 2006, 2007). Personal freedom thus often ends up being constrained, rather than being expanded, not only because of class-based unequal access to social resources, but also because personal success tends to be narrowly evaluated in terms of human capital and its market value, in particular through the accumulation of marketable skills (Urciuoli, 2008), given that neoliberalism is about the 'commodification of everything' (Harvey, 2005: 165).

These observations indicate that our critique of neoliberalism needs to be sensitive to social differentiation and stratification, and it is attention to people living in precarity (material, semiotic or psychological) that enables us to most forcefully critique neoliberalism. As I will show, the majority of adult English learners in this study were lower-middle-class working professionals from the Pearl River Delta, a region at the forefront of China's neoliberalization process (Ong, 2006); the English Corner in Yangshuo, located in close proximity to the region, makes it an important site to explore the dynamics between neoliberalism and language learning. Interviews with adult language learners in Yangshuo show that what appear to be naturally occurring conversations with foreigners actually involve reflexive thinking backstage (Goffman, 1959, 1963), which is aimed at the strategic management of interactions in the pursuit of English. The term 'interactional straining' is proposed to account for such management of interaction, that is, reflexive and strategic manipulation of interactional contents and/or structure so as to establish oneself as (pass for) a legitimate interlocutor. As I argue below, such interactional practice constitutes an important venue for examining the effects of neoliberal governmentality.

To briefly summarize, in examining this English Corner, my intention is not to evaluate its pedagogical effectiveness (see e.g. Krashen, 2006; Trottier, 2008) or to discuss the politics of authentic English (see e.g. Seargeant, 2005). Instead, through analyzing data from policy documents, participant observation and interviews, I examine how varied flows are managed in the development of the 'English Corner', what this construction of an English Corner says about the changing ideologies of English in China, how language learning proceeds in Yangshuo, and how some salient interactional practices can be conceptualized and explained.

English Educational Tourism and the FACES Method

The English language learning industry in Yangshuo is based on a folk language learning method – the 'FACES successful English learning method', developed by Zhang, a former tour guide. The idea of opening a language school first occurred to Zhang in the early 1990s. Through inviting foreign travelers to teach English, he opened the first private language school in 1993. The teaching combined classroom instruction with outdoor travel with international tourists, providing the students with more opportunities to practice their spoken English (summary notes from interview with Samuel[2]). The turning point came in 1997, when Li Yang, an English teacher who had already established his fame nationwide came to the City of Guilin to promote his 'Crazy English', a unique method of practicing spoken English by shouting out loud without fear of losing face (for details, see Bolton, 2003; Gao, 2012). Zhang was very eager to meet his entrepreneurial idol and they were later able to cooperatively hold the first English Summer Camp in Yangshuo in 1999. The celebrity effect of Li Yang and his 'Crazy English' helped Yangshuo gain fame almost overnight – a place to practice English with foreigners (*Yangshuo County Chronicles*, 2003).

This successful event prompted the government to start reconfiguring the significance of the private language education industry in Yangshuo against the backdrop of a more mature market economy and of changing ideologies of English in China, as I will elaborate later. Thus, despite having no academic background in English language education, Zhang managed to obtain support from the local government because of the great contribution his entrepreneurial initiative could make to the local economy. Different from the tentative approach taken in the early 1990s, the 1999 governmental plan explicitly stated that this very first private foreign language school should be strongly supported (*A Fast-Developing Tourism County*, 1999: 54–55). Under supportive government policies, more private language schools were then established. To attract international travelers to be English language teachers, schools put recruitment advertisements not only on their official websites, but also on popular backpacker websites such as Couchsurfing, or they simply advertised on the street (see Figure 5.3). Due to the temporariness of tourists' stay, local schools usually offer very flexible contracts. My interviews with foreign travelers show that they took up teaching positions mainly to support themselves financially while travelling around Yangshuo, though they may not have had equivalent teaching experience in their home countries, as Cathy explained:

Figure 5.3 A recruitment advertisement on the street (*Source*: Photo by author, 2011)

Extract 5.2

(Cathy, 29 years old, American)

I realize to stay, you have to make money ((laughter)) somehow, and have some way to pay for things ((laughter)) so I had thought a lot about teaching, because if I was a teacher then I could make some money and also stay in China. And I remember Yangshuo and how beautiful it was. So I just started to look on the internet for schools in Yangshuo, and [name of the school] came up((laughter)). … I knew that this was a nice city, and I knew that I would enjoy it, because I had already visited here. I wanted to go back to a city that is a little bit familiar to me, I like being outdoors, and being very active. I knew Yangshuo has a lot of activities, so.

This conforms with Uriely and Reichel's (2000: 270) observation that 'tourist-workers … share the tendency toward low spending as a result of their wish to experience long-term trip despite budget restrictions. In order to finance their prolonged trip, they also tend to engage in occasional and usually short-term employment during their trips. The jobs that they take are usually not related to their education, training, or skills. …Their involvement in these kinds of work is obviously not part of an occupational career. Yet, it is instrumental in terms of financing this touristic pursuit'. Thus, in this process, English in Yangshuo comes to acquire economic value, and English-speaking international tourists, embodying these valuable English resources, become moving subjects to be managed for the 'territorial concentrations of resources' (Sassen, 2002: 2, as cited in Hannam *et al.*, 2006: 7).

Naming this folk language learning method 'the FACES successful learning method', Zhang elaborated during an interview with a local radio station as follows:

Extract 5.3

My method is to ignore grammatical concepts like tense and others completely, and start straightaway from having conversations with foreigners. … We should not think of English as knowledge, but as an everyday skill – just like we don't really need to know about physics to learn to ride a bike. So my method can be called 'learning by doing', which is one important theory of the American pragmatist Dewey's. … Face means lian, mianzi. I must say we Chinese people have good English competence, and actually some are quite excellent. But we tend to be shy and dare not speak aloud. …we should not care so much about mianzi – just open your mouth even if you could make mistakes. So our

FACES learning method, to say it in English, is *I enjoy losing faces in order to leaning my English way* [sic].

Each character, as he further elaborated, stands for one sub-method of learning English:

F: Face to face with foreigners
A: Ask and answer
C: Change and change – change 1 sentence to 10 sentences; change short sentences to longer sentences
E: English to English
S: Swimming successfully

As we can see, English here is advocated as a 'skill' as opposed to 'knowledge'. This discourse of 'skill', abbreviated as FACES, makes it convenient to technologize and commodify English (Block, 2002; Kramsch, 2005) by erasing the complex social embeddedness of interactions (Gaudio, 2003), which in turn exacerbates potential tensions in actual interaction, as we shall see. The FACES method, therefore, reproduces the ideology of McCommunication (Block, 2002). Block (2002: 121) suggests that the widely observed tendency of 'treating ... communication as a set of technical skills that can be defined, made more efficient, quantified, predicted and ultimately controlled' can be termed 'McCommunication'. This term points to the existence of a frame which over-rationalizes communication, but also that this frame is commodified and spread around the world' (see also Pennycook [1994: 170–174] for ... a critique of communicative language teaching [CLT]).

It is this commodified and rationalized opportunity to speak with foreigners in order to practice English, as justified by the FACES method, that attracts students here. Indeed, at the school, there are no explicit guidelines as to how exactly students should approach foreigners and how to manage these conversations. Nevertheless, all 24 students, like the exemplary student Harry shown on the school's website, told me they would proactively seek opportunities to talk with foreigners. As Philip, an English language teacher from Canada, also observes about English learning here:

> if someone really wants to learn English, you have all the chance in the world to practice English, you know. You can go to a bar, you know, to chat with different kind of traveler every day, and at the school they can speak English 8 hours a day, even when outside the class, they speak

English with us, we speak English with them. So er it's a big opportunity for them.

While the absence of specific regulations seems to empower language learners ('you have all the chance in the world to practice English'), in reality it only intensifies the degree of self-control ('if someone really wants to') – a manifestation of the key paradox of neoliberal governmentality. In other words, the FACES method works by capitalizing on people's desires (Read, 2009) for authentic English and interaction, as opposed to merely sanctioning or regulating people's actual learning behavior. Therefore, the ideal learner is supposed to actively seek learning opportunities through self-governance (Olssen, 2006). How exactly learners conceptualize and manage interactions with foreigners becomes a key site where we can observe the effects of neoliberal governmentality.

So far, I have shown how international touristic flows are managed in the development of the 'English Corner' as part of the local tourism economy. However, the establishment of Yangshuo as an English Corner represents not just a business strategy. The commodification of English must also correspond to a market where English is in demand. Therefore, to understand the case of Yangshuo also requires understanding the larger contexts of the changing ideologies of English in China. Indeed, when talking with teachers about their students at the school, one recurring issue that teachers observed with great interest was how students ended up in Yangshuo learning English and what English meant to them. One of the teachers, David, said:

> I find their stories interesting. They came from all over China, you know, sometimes from far away, and they come here, often quit jobs, and come here to better their English, so I think that's interesting. It takes a lot of risk and commitment. And I respect that.

Peter, the most senior teacher in Samuel's, also testified to the career orientedness of Chinese students. He compared his Chinese students with the Japanese students he used to teach in Japan:

> I think, I think Chinese students seem to be more career-oriented. You know, in Japan, a lot of my students were, one of the questions I usually ask my students is why do they study English. Some of my adult students in Japan, you know, well, I'm bored, or I want to have a hobby, so I study English, or a common answer is like I want to travel. It will make

it easier to travel [see Kubota, 2011]. But like all of my students in China they say you know I want to get a better job.

So, what exactly does this construction of an English Corner say about the changing ideologies of English in China? The next section looks more specifically at who the students are and why they learn English against the larger context of a globalizing China.

English, Lifelong Learning and the Neoliberal Worker

Since the 1990s, China's growing integration with the global world has made the preparation of personnel with knowledge of business English an urgent issue. Against this context, communicative competence in English is specified as the main objective in a series of national English syllabuses issued in 1992, 1993 and 1996 (Hu, 2005: 10–11). Two national English tests, the Cambridge Business English Certificate (BEC) test and the China Public English Test System (PETS), with emphasis on business communication, were also introduced in 1993 and 1999, respectively, to be taken mainly by working professionals (Pang *et al.*, 2002). In 2001, just after Beijing won the bid for the 2008 Olympics, and just a few days before China officially became a member of the World Trade Organization (WTO), *People's Daily*, one of China's major newspapers, issued a report titled 'More Chinese Value Communication Skills'. As reported, Stephen E. Lucas, Professor of Communication Arts at the University of Wisconsin, arrived in Beijing to lecture on 'China, globalization and public speaking'. The participants were said to have acknowledged the need to learn 'Western-style communication skills'. 'As China remains the fastest-developing economic power worldwide', the article concluded, 'more Chinese people have to learn to voice their thoughts in a globally accepted way' (*People's Daily*, 2001).

With this rising importance of English for upward mobility in both education and work, there emerged a national craze for English. Private English language training centers started to appear and quickly expand under the market economy, catering to this increasing demand for English and making English language education a multibillion dollar industry (US$4.7 billion in 2010) (Bolton & Graddol, 2012: 3; see also Hu & McKay, 2012: 347; Wang, 2004). The privatization and industrialization of English language education has made English a commodity, further perpetuating the unequal access to English, which has become a marker of middle-class identity (Gao, 2012; Hu, 2005).

Notably, the need to improve one's English does not stop when one finishes education in the traditional sense. In recent years, Chinese working professionals find themselves caught up in the ever-increasing requirement for English, as documented in media reports (Yan, 2010; You, 2013), though little empirical research has been done (Bolton & Graddol, 2012: 7–8). In fact, the year after China joined the WTO, a society of lifelong learning (终身学习型社会) was put forward by the Communist Party of China (CPC) as an integral part of its goal to build a well-off (小康 xiǎokāng) society. Clearly, such objectives apply not only to institutional education per se, but also to the cultivation of human capital as proposed by Prime Minister Wu Yi in 2001 (Rofel, 2007: 173), that is, to 'allow superior talent to be distinguished' and 'give free rein to people's capabilities'. Similar to what has been observed in Europe, neoliberalism in China pertains to the way economics, knowledge and learning interact (Olssen, 2006: 217; Ong, 2006; Yan, 2003). The cultivation of human capital through lifelong learning represents what Olssen (2006: 224) calls 'internalized educational aspiration', so that 'essentially the learner becomes the entrepreneurs of their own development'. Against this national context, English language learning has become the key site where we can observe the effects of neoliberalism.

Indeed, contrary to what is usually expected of an exam-oriented society, in particular when it comes to learning English (Pan & Block, 2011), the English language learning program in Yangshuo emphatically defines its objective in the following way:

> the purpose of coming to our school should be to quickly improve your language use skills, like speaking, listening, communicating etc. within a short period of time; If you simply want to improve your grammar or test-taking skills, just don't come.

Almost all the students[3] I interviewed are working professionals in companies with international businesses, and 17 of them are from Guangdong Province, Guangxi's neighboring province. They may or may not have college degrees and most are actually working migrants in economically vibrant and competitive cities in southern China. All of them had either left or were intending to change their jobs when deciding to come to learn English. With years of working experience, the working professionals' decision to learn English represents a calculated choice and a reflexive decision in relation to the dynamism of the global economy and the labor market (Ong, 2007: 4–5). Jon explained to me why he quit his job to learn English:

Extract 5.4

(Jon, 36 years old, used to be a salesperson in Guangdong; had been studying in Yangshuo for seven months)

...because it's not easy to get more order in the market now... because it is difficult time for many companies. Maybe in this financial crisis, many companies meet, meet, er, er, this difficulty, so I think I must I have to learn something to improve myself, and looking for another job.

Such discourse on increasing one's employability through English learning was also echoed by other participants, as they looked forward to 'the promise of English' (Park, 2011), that is, a better job with higher pay:

Extract 5.5

(Zed, 25 years old, car parts production supervisor, worked in Hunan, had been studying in Yangshuo for more than one year)

...actually that's why I quitted the job. I didn't pass the exam for the job promotion. I was the supervisor in the department, and I had to pass the exam to become the manager. I didn't pass the exam. [The exam] it's about knowledge, and relationship, and professional skills, and also English. Because they used English for the interview, every part I did a good job, but interview it's very bad. ...They have three men [examiners], they asked me many questions about cars, my hobbies, and something. I didn't answer [well], because I didn't know their meanings. It was not very difficult questions.

Extract 5.6

(Tina, 22 years old, salesperson working in Guangdong; had been studying in Yangshuo for two months)

I want to change another job. They want PETS-4.[7] I have no choice.... I still want to do international business. [But] I want to be a manager, not just a staff. I don't always be a staff or worker. If I learn English well, I get promotion.... I have to improve myself.

As Tina and Zed explained, English has become an important part of human capital and a gate-keeping language in global workplaces in

China, and their pursuit of English is largely motivated by the need, if not the imperative ('I have no choice'), for self-improvement.

For all my student participants then, learning English is supposed to better prepare them in the increasingly competitive job market in China. In the transformative turn from the planned to a market economy, the assignment system, wherein people's work would be assigned by the state as an 'iron rice bowl' (lifelong tenured job), was gradually replaced in the late 1990s by a labor market, which meant that, for the first time, people were encouraged to work for a workplace and in a position of their own choice (see Hoffman, 2010). But the most extensive changes came after Deng Xiaoping's South China Tour in 1992 (Bian, 2009). The 1992 South China Tour was meant to open China to the market economy through neoliberalism as exception (Ong, 2006), and it was at this time that Deng Xiaoping made his famous remark that 'to be rich is glorious', remanaging the population by fostering self-actualizing or self-enterprising subjects (Ong, 2007: 5). This year marked the beginning of unprecedented mobility in China, both intercity and rural–urban, with people plunging into the sea of the market, and layoffs becoming the societal routine (Bian, 2009: 177).

It is in this historical process that we see the growth of Chinese professionals, who constitute the emerging Chinese middle class, as both the key players in the rising market economy and the most direct targets of neoliberal thinking, with constant pressure to become 'educated and self-managing citizens who can compete in global knowledge markets' (Ong, 2007: 6). 'Neoliberalism's metaphor', as Ong (2007: 5) sharply and succinctly points out, 'is knowledge', defined as those skills that can generate economic returns. Under the dual pressure of job insecurity and the constant need for self-improvement, Chinese working professionals are supposed to practice 'self-enterprise and self-reflexivity in the face of market uncertainty' (Ong, 2008: 184), and even have to take further risks, including quitting their job to learn English, the language that defines what 'success' means under globalization, as put forward by the school's slogan 'success in English, success in life' (see Figure 5.4; see also Blommaert, 2010: 55–56).

However, English not only supposedly helps increase the chance of upward mobility; good English has also become almost iconic

Figure 5.4 'Success in English, success in life' (*Source*: Photo by author, 2011)

(Irvine & Gal, 2000) of professionalism, the lack of which could even become a target of contempt. For instance, Amy, with almost 10 years' working experience, was already a manager in charge of her company's business transactions with about 19 countries. She nevertheless quit her job, not just because of her incompetence in English, but also because this had led to disrespect from her employees. Below is what she said when I asked her why she wanted to learn English:

Extract 5.7

(Amy, 30 years old, manager of a company in Guangdong; had been studying in Yangshuo for about 10 months)

Because I want to be 名正言顺的经理 [*a manager in the real sense of the word*]. No complaints from my employees. Sometimes my assistants would compare with me in a quite sensational way. Just like, why you don't know English and you can get higher salary than us? And if I let them do the translation, 有时候假装没听到，尤其是pay day [*they sometimes pretended they didn't hear me, especially when it was the pay day*]. I can feel that. Sometimes I asked them to do some extra work, they refused me. They said 'I don't like to work overtime, because my salary is too low, my position is low, you can do it, don't ask us'.

For Amy, her weaker English language competence compared to that of her subordinates is not simply a practical problem that interferes with her job performance as a manager, but it is also an issue of professionalism, which ultimately leads her to question whether she is 'a manager in the real sense of the word'. Through improving English, she said '[I hope to] do my future work well without translators. If I have a high position, I also need an assistant, but not for translating'. Therefore, while having an administrative assistant testifies to Amy's high professional position as a manager, having a language assistant, or translator, only undermines her professionalism. In this way, the English language is naturalized as an indispensable component of the ideal professional identity, and investment in English is internalized as a moral issue. A good command of English not only helps improve work efficiency, but more importantly, authenticates a professional identity through the demonstration of English as proof of legitimacy, credibility and authority (c.f. Wee, 2008: 261–264). Amy's bold move to quit her job and invest time and money in learning English is precisely a way of realigning herself with this neoliberal ideal, as it positions her as willingly taking risks to improve her English rather than remaining secluded in her already achieved position as a manager. It is in this context that Chinese working professionals in the present research started their quest for English.

Talking to Foreigners around Town

Intrusive exploitations of interaction: Foreigners' perspectives

Based on my interviews and observations, there are three public places in Yangshuo where foreigners tend to predominate, and also where interactions between foreigners and students could be frequently observed: school areas, business streets and bars (or similar establishments).

Peter came from the United States and, of all the teachers I knew, he had worked at Samuel's for the longest period of time (about two years). He explained at length about the popularity of Yangshuo and how talking with many foreigners here was like 'immersion learning'. Nevertheless, when asked about his own experience of talking to people on the street, Peter framed it in a different way:

> Well, usually I don't have time, right, and I would say I'm sorry but I'm going somewhere, sorry I can't. ...But, to be honest, I don't think I'm not a very outgoing kind of person. ...I'm usually not really excited. ...I don't usually have conversations like this, with er people who want to practise English.

Here, Peter first said he could not have such conversations because he was usually quite busy, which turned out to be a polite excuse when he added that a more honest reason was that he was not outgoing. Such self-exclusion as a potential interlocutor with English learners, however, was not just a matter of temperament ('outgoing' or not), as Peter himself claimed. As I found out, since foreigners are constantly approached for a talk in English, many of them, like Peter, have learned to avoid such conversations that, according to their own accounts, tend to be repetitive, simple and boring.

Thus, exactly what kind of interactions do students and teachers have, and why would teachers tend to avoid such interactions?

One afternoon, I was sitting on a bench outside the school building, having a chat with a couple of teachers. Several students walked out of the building and eagerly 'helloed' to join the conversation. 'Not a moment's break', Philip whispered helplessly to another teacher, Sam. When the students came over and sat down, one of them asked Sam in not very fluent English, 'Are you a new teacher? Because I haven't seen you before'. 'I've been here for about one week', he replied, 'and you?'. 'I am an old student. I have been here for for three three three weeks'. Obviously, she was searching for the word 'week'. 'I thought you were going to say three months', he looked at Philip and they grinned at each other (Field note, 8 July 2011). Seeing this, I was reminded of the interview I had with Sam several days earlier (4 July 2011). Reflecting on his experience of being approached just for a talk in English, he said:

Extract 5.8

Sometimes talking to a person with low English competence can be stressful. You have to change your mind a little bit. You know, you have to think slower, and talk slower, and listen very carefully, and it's like teaching, you know. Sometimes you feel like if you get paid.

As he finished, he looked at me with an awkward smile. On the one hand, he did teach at the language school and got paid for his work. Yet, on the other hand, being constantly approached for a talk in English outside his official teaching hours made him feel that he was being unreasonably exploited for his linguistic capital. Adjusting to the interlocutor's pace of talk ('think slower, talk slower'), being more attentive ('listen very carefully') and spending greater efforts to figure out meanings of interaction ('change your mind a little bit'), these otherwise unnecessary accommodations make interacting with students seem like doing extra work without payment ('sometimes you feel like if you get paid').

This is not to say that interactions between students and teachers could never be pleasant. During social night events, for instance, I observed students and teachers interact and even pose for photos together. These happy moments are also published on the school's website. My initial thought on the social events was that it was nice that the school organized these varied kinds of activities. At least, compared with lessons inside the classrooms, these activities, such as quizzes, speech competitions and singing competitions, seemed to be more interesting activities for both the students and the teachers. Or, that is what I assumed.

One day after school, I was sitting by the river with Philip, and somehow (or maybe intentionally on my part) we started chatting about his work at the school. At one point, I mentioned that the school seemed to have many interesting activities, like the social night. On hearing this, he immediately gave me a serious look and asked rhetorically 'what do you think the social night is about?'. 'It's just for the students to have more chance to speak with foreigners, you know', he answered himself in a complaining tone. 'All the students come to you and talk. The school just wants to make them happy. That's the secret!' (Field note, 9 July 2011). Indeed, immediately after my interview with Peter, I asked whether he was going upstairs to the social night. 'Yes, I will', he replied. As he finished his banana and threw the peel into the wastebasket, he added, 'you know, I wanted to start our interview earlier because they [the school] just told me this afternoon, they want me to be the judge of the speech competition [the theme of that day's social night]. I definitely wouldn't go if they hadn't asked me' (Field note, 14 July 2011).

As we can see, putting on a good face and actively interacting with students is the inevitable cost that these foreign teachers have to pay for utilizing their own linguistic capital as English teachers. However, the school area is not the only place where students seek out learning opportunities. Business streets and bars are actually more popular among students. Even in their personal time when socializing in bars, foreign teachers tend to be constantly disturbed by conversation seekers. In the following extract, Steve, from Ireland, raised the issue of always 'bumping into' students at bars:

> Of course, you are always, I mean, you gonna talk to people [at bars], and chances are that some of them are going to be students… Er, yeah, that's fine maybe. I mean … you bumped into them, or after school you see them there. …I've talked to so many. …maybe they've got very little English, or maybe they are just repeating themselves, of course, that's boring. I don't want to, it's now my social time. I have got no time teaching them English, so people like them, you know, I'll just finish the conversation, and talk to my friends or someone else.

Here, Steve actually first attempted to avoid directly answering my question by invoking my Chinese identity ('I am talking to one now') in a joking manner, and then providing a more or less neutral answer 'that's fine maybe'. But after further inquiries, he acknowledged that while there might be interesting conversations wherein 'you can have a laugh you can have a joke', he had also 'talked to so many' who 'got very little English' and kept 'repeating themselves'. In such situations, he would thus have to try to exit the conversations to safeguard his own social time ('it's now my social time. I have got no time teaching them English' 'it's my time off, I'm gonna have fun').

So, on the one hand, we see that for foreign teachers, their English acquires economic value in this English Corner that might not be available to them in their home countries (Blommaert *et al.*, 2005; Cho, 2012), and they can take on English teaching jobs to finance their touristic interests in Yangshuo. But on the other hand, control of their own linguistic capital is limited in certain ways, because they constantly have to deal with students both around and outside the campus who want to practice English with them. Making the effort either to patiently try to understand their interlocutors or to find an exit from undesirable conversations thus becomes an inherent dilemma involved in optimizing their own linguistic capital.

However, basically any place that is popular among foreigners tends to attract students. Kay was from South Africa. Like other local foreigners, he took a job as an English teacher when he first arrived, but now he was running his own coffee shop. He said he had been stopped on the street for a talk in English so 'many times' that he had learned to avoid such 'attempts to create interactions' that might be full of repetitive simple questions ('where are you from? do you like China? how many cities have you been to in China? how many countries have you been to?'). While these pseudo-attempts at interaction ('please write your name, your email, maybe and little comments') or repetitive simple questions on the street make talking with students rather dull and boring, there are also other concerns for him. Since he runs the coffee shop, regular customers also come and speak to him 'just as a foreigner'; some have even offered to work for him for free, as he explained:

> Generally they work here more to practice their English than to earn money. A lot of, a lot of students in Yangshuo work at, work at bars, work at restaurants because they just want to be in a place where people do speak English. They want to be here because I always speak English, because customers speak English. It's good, it's just practice for their English.

While free labor seemed good, Kay said that this actually didn't work well because 'they only want to do the nice work, they don't want to do the bad work. They don't want to wash the cups. They only want to make the coffees, and serve the customers'.

As we have seen, foreigners were not always ready to talk with students, and would try to find ways to avoid such interactions. Talking to foreigners, therefore, would not happen as easily and conveniently as the FACES method prescribes and promises. Indeed, conversations never occur naturally but have constraints – the social situatedness and embeddedness of interactions as well as the necessary language competence required mean that there are always minimum conditions to be met for interactions to occur in the first place (see Gaudio, 2003 for details;

Goffman, 1959). Successfully managing such conditions, therefore, could be vital for students to have actual access to authentic English and interaction. However, as already mentioned, the technologization of English as a 'skill' meant that knowledge of English and communication was discarded as irrelevant and not taught in schools. Adult students would thus have to find their own ways of approaching and talking to foreigners. As we shall see, the students did not complain about insufficient institutional support or the false promise of the FACES method. Rather, they became proactive learners who were managers of their own self-development (Olssen, 2006): they showed their initiative, reflected upon the difficulties and internalized such constraints as problems to be tackled on their own.

Excitements, frustrations and strategies: Students' perspectives

In stark contrast to foreigners who may well dismiss such interactions as simple and boring, adult students told me how complex talking to foreigners can actually be for them – there were moments of frustration as well as excitement, and they had to actively seek out strategies to preempt and mitigate potential tensions in interaction.

Mary had studied at Samuel's for about six months, and described her feelings when talking to foreigners as both 'nervous' and 'exciting'. She told me that she was often 'nervous' about not being able to express herself fluently in English ('just one word, one word, very slowly'), but was excited to have found an Australian friend with whom she was still in touch via Skype. Hearing this, I congratulated her on having found a friend to practice her English, but she added regrettably:

Extract 5.9

(Interview with Mary, 27 years old, salesperson and human resource personnel working in Guangdong; had been studying in Yangshuo for half a year)

...but sometimes I can't find the topic to talk, half an hour, and don't know how to continue.

[And there're] many times because they know we want to practice our English, so they go away.

Here, Mary hoped to be able to carry on longer conversations, and identified the problem as not being able to find enough topics. Also, she revealed that she might not be taken as a legitimate interlocutor because of her weak competence in English ('they know we want to practice our

English, so they go away'). Similarly, another student Tina, a salesperson from Guangdong, told me that because she did not always know what to talk about, 'they [foreigners] will feel very boring, and go away... I think it's very embarrassing, because we can't communicate with them, oh my God, what a pity, because we want so much to talk with them'.

We see that adult students were aware that they might come across as nuisances to foreigners ('they will feel very boring, and go away'). However, they did not see the problems and difficulties as deriving from the false promise of the FACES method; instead, they blamed themselves for not always being able to initiate or sustain conversations ('it's very embarrassing', 'what a pity') and yet still showed their perseverance. In order to be able to speak with foreigners, they tried to overcome their nervousness and identify possible reasons for being ignored. In other words, students internalized the interactional tensions and constraints, which have been exacerbated by the neoliberal enterprise of language commodification in Yangshuo, and at the same time were persistent and proactive in finding ways to mitigate such tensions so as to pass for legitimate interlocutors – a key manifestation of the dynamic relationship between neoliberalism and active learning (Olssen, 2006). For example, Lora had devised a seemingly passive way to improve her English, as she explained:

Extract 5.10

(Lora, 24 years old, logistics worker in Guangdong, planning to be a salesperson; had been studying in Yangshuo for four months)

When I went [name] bar, I just sat there quietly and listen to others, classmate. Said nothing. I didn't say anything. ...even though I can't speak, but I can listen, I believe several times later you can speak and your listening will be better.

For Lora, being silent does not mean being uninterested. Indeed, if we rely on recordings of interactions alone, people like Lora may well be left out of the analysis because she had no voice. Nevertheless, as she explained, not talking does not mean relinquishing the opportunity to improve her English; rather, it is a self-initiated strategy based on her reflexive understanding of learning (listening first, speaking later), so that ultimately one can speak out. Another student, Carl, told me how he and his friends managed to find the 'right' foreigners to talk with:

Extract 5.11

(Carl, 28 years old, business owner from Guangdong, had been studying in Yangshuo for two months)

I think foreigners em like beer, er he he usually oftenly sit in bar, er only drink beer... I usually go to bar, conversation with foreigner... I came with my friends, four or three together... if I I only talk with foreigner, er, ((laughter)) I I speak a little time, I talked a little time 只能说一会，然后就没什么说的了，一般是3、4个人一起，这个不会那个说一下，这样会时间长一点吧，如果我一个人在那跟他说的话，说两句，不知道说哪里去 ((laughter)) [*I can only speak for a little while, and then have nothing to say. So usually we three or four people go together. If one person doesn't know what to say, then another person can try to say something. This way, we can talk for a longer time. If I were there alone talking with him, maybe after two sentences, I don't know what to say next ((laughter))*] ... If many people together, 我不会过去 [*I won't go*], if em, he only sit one there, em maybe ((laughter)) talk with foreigner.

Like many other students, Carl went to places popular among foreigners (bars), but he also opted for the strategy of finding foreigners sitting alone, who tended to be more approachable than those hanging out with friends. And he would go together with many Chinese friends so that there was always someone to fill in otherwise embarrassing silences. These strategies showed that Carl took the initiative and came up with strategies to turn potentially boring and fallible conversations into successful and more interesting ones. Another student, Lucy, planned to work in Yangshuo after finishing her study at the school:

Extract 5.12

(Lucy, 28 years old, housewife, planning to look for a job; had been studying in Yangshuo for five months)

...after I study here, maybe I will find a part-time job here at some beer bar, about one month or two months, just to practice my oral English, and then go back to my home, find a good job... because you know... the foreigner customer want to buy something, you can communicate with them.

Here, we see that students are eager to practice their English but at the same time are constantly frustrated by an inability to sustain long conversations, or simply by being ignored by foreigners. However, some students tackled these difficulties by strategically manipulating the structure of the conversation, that is, multiple people engaging in conversations with solo travelers, or adopting the more passive role of a quiet listener so as to improve listening over time, or even taking a different method by working on West Street.

Talking to Foreigners: A Precarious Genre

So far, I have described how the so-called 'biggest English Corner in China' was established and how it works. Based on a folk method called the 'FACES successful English learning method', this English Corner gained popularity by providing an otherwise unavailable opportunity to practice English with foreigners. I have also shown that interactions between foreigners and language learners often involve tension for both parties. On the one hand, foreigners who felt that the conversation was too simple and boring, and would find ways to end the conversation or, as they learned better, would simply keep students at bay, in order to avoid being exploited of their linguistic capital. On the other hand, students would find ways to talk with foreigners, and failing to do so would result in regrets and self-blame. In this constant search for an exit by one conversational party and the persistent effort to engage in conversation by the other, we see the clashing efforts that each party makes in negotiating or manipulating potential interaction, with one strategically entering into and sustaining conversation while the other might attempt to avoid and exit from the encounter, regardless of whether a conversation actually occurs (ignored or not), how it proceeds (boring or not) and how it ends (sustained or not). There is an obvious mismatch, though students can also successfully pass as legitimate interlocutors on some occasions. So, how to make sense of this tension? And how such interactional straining is related to the image of an entrepreneurial self for these working professionals?

First, claiming that students have poor linguistic competence provides only a partial explanation. While some students do need to look for the right expressions or have to repeat themselves, there are also cases when students can somehow sustain conversations for a period of time, according to both foreigners and the students themselves (e.g. see Extract 5.11). Actually, some students who arrived with little English told me that they would only start looking for foreigners to talk with after learning more English. Also, saying that students have poor social skills fails to account for the fact that some students are well aware that 'they may feel we are boring' (e.g. Extract 5.9), and some are able to come up with strategies to avoid potential interactional breakdowns (e.g. Extracts 5.11 and 5.12). The tension involved in these conversations, I would suggest, arises from the different ways the interlocutors involved conceptualize the potential interactions at hand, including what topic might be relevant (e.g. Extracts 5.9 and 5.11), how the conversation should proceed (e.g. Extract 5.11) and most important of all, what the purposes of these interactions are (e.g. Extract 5.9). We have seen that for foreigners, socializing around Yangshuo in their private free time means having fun and enjoying themselves, or in the case of Kay, casually talking with customers is part of his business life. But for students, hanging out with foreigners is less about simply relaxing and having fun, and more about strategically exploiting the opportunities to practice spoken English under the guise of a casual talk.

All in all, as we have seen, talking to foreigners turns out to be a precarious genre. We see that students are eager to practice their English but may have difficulty sustaining or even starting conversations. However, they are not easily deterred by these difficulties, nor do they complain about the FACES method. Actually, despite these difficulties and constraints, the students internalized these problems as something to be worked out on their own, and tried to adopt various strategies to create interactional opportunities and/or manipulate potential interactional structures, for example, by choosing the place of interaction (going to bars and shops popular among foreigners), purposefully selecting the participants and managing the topics of interaction (multiple people engaging in conversations with solo travelers) and designing one's roles during interaction (being a quiet listener or working in a local shop). Through using these tactics based on their own reflexive thinking, they exemplify the image of an ideal neoliberal self (Foucault, 1991) who, instead of passively relying on external support, shows self-discipline, internalizes constraints on themselves and exhibits reflexivity and calculated thinking to make an unfavorable learning environment work for their own purpose.

In other words, the legitimacy of such interactions needs to be constantly negotiated, established and maintained. In order to practice English, students had to carefully manage the accessibility of foreigners, exploit opportunities amid constraints and skillfully sustain the conversation, so as to preempt possible avoidance. This informal way of learning English differs from English learning within formal educational institutions in China, wherein learning tends to be exam-oriented and the learning process subjected to regimented procedures and guidelines (Pan & Block, 2011; Peréz-Milans 2013). Learning English in Yangshuo corresponds more to the model of a proactive and self-responsible learner, for whom the neoliberal logic of autonomy, self-improvement and self-governance is incorporated into their everyday learning process (Olssen, 2006).

It is worth noting that such interactional precarity derives not from crosstalk, that is, a misunderstanding or a breakdown in cross-cultural communication (c.f. Gumperz *et al.*, 1981), but from the technologization and commodification of English that erases the social embeddedness of interactions, thereby exacerbating potential interactional constraints and tensions as language learners pursue the valuable linguistic capital of English. Their involvement in and navigation of the tensions show that they are knowing subjects who, despite potential ambivalence and constraints, work out strategies and take the initiative for self-care and personal development (Foucault, 1988; Ong, 2007, 2008). Therefore, as they seek to explore these language learning opportunities amid constraints in this English Corner, the students exemplify proactive English learning, an essential aspect of the technologies of the self (Foucault, 1988). In other words, these language learners are caught up in this neoliberal enterprise and have to constantly reflect on potential interactions, including what topic might be relevant (e.g. Extract 5.5), how the conversation should proceed (e.g. Extract 5.7), as well as overcoming anxieties (e.g. Extract 5.5). What appear to be naturally occurring conversations with foreigners involve reflexive thinking backstage (Goffman, 1959, 1963). The term 'interactional straining' is proposed to account for such manipulation of interaction, that is, reflexive and strategic manipulation of interactional contents and/or structure so as to establish oneself as (pass for) a legitimate interlocutor. Interactional straining, as documented in this study, provides a key site to observe the dynamic relationships between language and neoliberalism as it is embedded in the active and yet contentious pursuit of linguistic capital and the cultivation of human capital under the neoliberal regime.

Specifically, interactional straining involves both subjective and semiotic processes of managing conversations. On the semiotic level, it can be understood as a deliberative interactional practice based on a particular language ideology, that is, 'conceptions of ... the nature and purpose of communication and of communicative behavior as an enactment of a collective order' (Silverstein, 1987: 1–2, as cited in Woolard, 1992), the collective order here being neoliberal governmentality. Without explicit instructions or guidelines, the adult students in the present study showed their initiative in language learning and self-development through actively designing and manipulating interactional contents and structure. On the subjective level, it also indicates that there were mixed emotions and anxieties as students tried to align themselves with the role of a legitimate interlocutor, instead of being merely a learner of English. Neoliberalism shapes, not determines, subjectivity – the ideal image of the neoliberal self is not seamlessly reproduced without struggles. There are always tensions in negotiating or manipulating potential interactions, regardless of whether the interaction actually occurs (ignored or not), how it proceeds (boring or not) and how it ends (sustained or not). As the lower-middle-class working professionals align themselves with the ideal image of a neoliberal self, they are caught up in a precarious process of strategically exploring interactional opportunities amid constraints, and skillfully sustaining conversations so as to become legitimate interlocutors for the purpose of language learning.

Summary

In this chapter, I have shown how the English language in Yangshuo has come to acquire economic value in the turn toward a market economy. From the establishment of the first private language school in 1993 to what is now said to be the 'biggest English Corner' in China, Yangshuo has been experimenting with commodifying English and mobilizing internaional travelers who embody the valuable resource of English. Learning English in Yangshuo is justified through a widely mediatized folk language method, the so-called FACES successful learning method, and its popularity corresponds to the changing ideologies of English in a globalizing China where English is becoming an index of middle-class professional identity. Specifically, the language learners come from southern China and work in lower-middle-class positions in small-scale international companies; they are working hard to prove their English so as to increase their competitiveness in the job market.

I have shown that the seemingly endless opportunities to interact with foreigners, anywhere and anytime in Yangshuo, are actually constrained. Foreigners might find the conversation too simple, repetitive or boring to be continued, or as they know better, might simply try to avoid such interactions; students, on the other hand, have learned to come up with strategies to initiate or sustain conversations. This constant manipulation of interaction is what I have called 'interactional straining'. Being a proactive English learner by seeking and utilizing interactional opportunities amid constraints in Yangshuo, the students correspond to an image of the neoliberal self who makes calculated decisions, takes initiatives and risks, and explores opportunities for self-improvement.

Notes

(1) College English Test, Band 6.
(2) Samuel is the principal of Samuel Language School, and turns out to be Zhang's brother. English pseudonyms are used for the school principal and students, because it is the general practice for everyone at the school to be addressed by an English name.
(3) The only exception was Lucy. She was learning English to prepare herself for the job market after several years of being a housewife.

6 Globalization: A Short Reflection

The aim of this book has been to examine the dynamics between language and social change at the tourism site of West Street, Yangshuo, so as to contribute to our understanding of the sociolinguistics of globalization. Through examining the tourism site as a social field (Leite & Graburn, 2009: 37) wherein tourist mobilities are embedded in and interact with historical, geographical, social, cultural, economic and semiotic factors, I have investigated various material and semiotic processes involved in the social change of West Street and their effects on people's everyday lives in the 'global village'. Specifically, the establishment of the 'global village' is an economic development strategy and also a cultural image produced in tourism promotional discourses. In this process, multiple tourism mobilities are appropriated and capitalized on as symbolic opportunities (Blommaert, 2010) for branding the place as a 'global village' and an 'English Corner'. Throughout the book, I have also underscored the importance of examining the contingent unfolding of local histories, paying attention to how local changes only emerge at the nexus of local, national and global forces. The transformation of West Street is deeply embedded in the transformation of Chinese society under globalization. Also, the process of social change is not free from tensions or struggles. Nor is the process finished: the story told here at best captures a historical moment still in change.

In examining the above issues, I have looked at data collected from multiple sources including online tourism promotional discourses, tourist writings, policy documents and relevant written literature, ethnographic interviews and observations. These data provide multiple perspectives on the sociohistorical transformation of West Street, Yangshuo, and reflect my own journey of learning and problem-solving (Erickson, 1986: 140) as a researcher. I hope I have shown that as we face the challenges of globalization for sociolinguistic research (Blommaert, 2010; Bucholtz,

2003; Eckert, 2003) and try to understand the various flows and inter-connectivities under globalization, a particular locale, the traditional unit of sociolinguistic and linguistic anthropological research, still matters. As Rampton (2000: 16) argues, 'community level studies... remain essential'. This is also the perspective adopted by Blommaert (2010), as he notes:

> ...I have often focused on the periphery as the locus from which we need to look at globalization. This, I believe, is essential: part of the shift we need to make is also a shift away from a metropolitan perspective on globalization, stressing the uniformity of such processes, towards a perspective that does justice to 'vernacular globalization', to the myriad ways in which global processes entre local conditions and circumstances and become a localized reality. (Blommaert, 2010: 197)

In other words, attention to the interdependence and interaction between local and non-local factors can help us appreciate and understand the myriad and often unexpected ways that vernacular globalization takes place.

Examining the 'global village' at the local–national–global nexus, I showed in Chapter 3 that the branding of West Street as a 'global village' and 'English Corner' for domestic Chinese tourists involves the appropriation and commodification of English. Such strategic mobilization of resources reproduces ideologies of English in China as a status marker, but it also generates ideological tensions. While some domestic Chinese tourists show their alignment with the idea of English as a middle-class identity marker, other tourists are contemptuous of such ideas, seeing them as superficial, pretentious and consumeristic. The transformation of West Street is also examined through looking at the spatial dynamics and tensions. In Chapter 4, I showed that this process involves demographic, geographical and semiotic reconfigurations of the local street and creates tensions among different groups of people who are variously positioned to social change. Interviews with the first-wave businesspersons and the local foreigners indicate that the 'global village' is not a space of frictionless flows; rather, it excludes and marginalizes certain people and social practices.

The tensions were further explored in Chapter 5 where I looked at English educational tourism. I showed that the promotion of the place as an 'English Corner' has been attracting working professionals from neighboring provinces. The social significance of English within the Chinese context means that English has great importance for upward mobility in the job market. These working professionals are attracted to Yangshuo for this otherwise unavailable and unaffordable opportunity to interact and practice English with English-speaking foreigners. Examining this interactional activity from the perspectives of both language learners and foreigners, I showed that there are always tensions in interaction, with language learners strategically exploring opportunities to initiate and maintain conversations while being shunned by foreigners. I suggest that by navigating themselves among ambivalence and constraints, the working professionals exemplify what is meant by technology of self in neoliberalizing China.

Overall, the transformation of West Street, Yangshuo, from a traditional neighborhood into a 'global village' capitalizes on the emerging Chinese consumer culture characterized by conspicuous consumption and a quest for modernity. The English language as one semiotic resource is appropriated and mobilized for such purposes; nevertheless, it is also caught up in tensions among different social groups. In the following sections, I discuss the methodological and theoretical implications of the research.

Methodological Reflections

In Chapter 2, I explained the issues of research methods and field access, as well as constraints during fieldwork. However, since the same research methods and techniques can be used by researchers with different assumptions in knowledge production (Erickson, 1986: 119–120; Rampton, 2006: 387), it is important to make clear how exactly I approached the research site, and how various data became useful evidence for constructing particular arguments about language and social change.

• Complexity

My research site is a place of constant change and transformations wherein varied mobilities have rendered invalid many assumptions about community (see Chapter 1). An ethnographic approach that could capture the complexity of the field was therefore adopted (Blommaert, 2007a; Blommaert & Dong, 2010; Blommaert & Rampton, 2011). Whereas in many other approaches, several variables might be predefined and/or controlled so as to be tested for correlational results, ethnography aims to capture social life as it is (Blommaert & Dong, 2010: 11–12; Rampton, 2006: 385). Actually, 'if [ethnographic] fieldwork doesn't start from assumptions of complexity', as Blommaert and Dong (2010: 86) put it, 'it is bound to miss the whole point'.

It is this openness of ethnography to everyday life that differentiates it from many other approaches. However, as Hymes (1996: 7) clearly states, 'all this is not to say that ethnography is open-minded to the extent of being empty-minded, that ignorance and naiveté are wanted'. The starting point in this open-minded quest to understand complexity is to get to know the research site *critically*. Hymes (1996: 7) states that, 'the more the ethnographer knows on entering the field, the better the result is likely to be. Training for ethnography is only partly a matter of training for getting information and getting along. It is also a matter of providing a systematic knowledge of what is known so far about the subject' (see also Blommaert & Dong, 2010; Erickson, 1986; Heath & Street, 2008). Therefore, pre-fieldwork preparation involves getting to know as much as possible about the field, particularly through adequate contextualization of the research site (Blommaert & Dong, 2010: 17–18). In my pre-field preparation, I made use of online news reports, tourism websites, tourist writings and guidebooks, as well as other historical documents/records available in library archives, to gain as much knowledge as possible about the relevant social, historical, economic and cultural aspects of Yangshuo and of China in general.

Prior knowledge may trigger questions that are worth exploring in the field, as shown in Chapter 2. Also, it is important to critically engage with what seems to be established facts and hold them in check during fieldwork. As we have seen, media discourses naturalize an iconic relationship between English and globality (see Chapter 3), erase the historical process of mobilization and present instead an image of the 'global village' wherein local tradition and history are completely absent. It is through deconstructing the material and semiotic processes involved that we see the more complex processes which are erased and simplified in public discourses. In this sense, ethnographic work can help 'challenge and critique established views' (Blommaert & Dong, 2010: 10–12).

We also uncovered the complexity of interaction in Chapter 5. Here, interaction and language learning is simplified and technologized as a FACES method in public promotional discourses: students happily talk with foreigners over beer, improving their English without even realizing it. It is through examining interview data as meta-discourse on interaction that we see how complex interaction actually is. Language learners and foreigners rarely, if ever, talk on the same page. Here, we see how interactions in the foreground actually involve background (Goffman, 1963) manipulation of the interaction in terms of its structure, content, pace, participation framework, etc. In explaining how they approach foreigners for a talk, language learners show that they are proactive learners who draw upon their own grassroots reflective knowledge of interaction, which, quite interestingly, echoes some well-established insights into the social embeddedness of interaction. For example, bars can be popular places for approaching foreigners (c.f. Goffman, 1963: 22: physical co-presence in public places makes people accessible to each other for potential interaction); creating interactional opportunities for language learning (c.f. Goffman, 1963: 139: possible gains from engaging in conversations may well encourage people to adopt strategies so as to accomplish uninformed ends); and also, the same genre can always be used for different purposes (when students choose to work in a bar, serving customers then becomes an easily accessible chance to speak and practice their English). As Bauman (1999: 86) observes, 'certain genres may become the object of special ideological focus'.

- Nativeness

It is therefore important to find out the native's viewpoints, instead of relying solely on existing published materials or documents. Indeed, the validity of ethnographic inquiries also depends on accurately capturing 'the meanings of behaviors and institutions to those who participate in them' (Hymes, 1996: 8; see also Erickson, 1986: 119–120).

Two main methods used to capture the local meanings in the present research were interview and observation. Specifically, I chose to use semi-structured qualitative interviews for this study. This type of interview is more of an exploratory and interactional nature, wherein the interview is conducted along certain themes or topics but always in a conversational manner to elicit viewpoints, stories and unexpected anecdotes (Blommaert & Dong, 2010: 46–47). Therefore, the questions I prepared served more as a rough guideline than a schedule to be strictly followed. This type of interview is appropriate for ethnographic research wherein participants' viewpoints are valued (Warren, 2001: 85).

At the same time, as Hymes (1996: 8) cautions, 'all this is not to say that members of a community themselves have an adequate model of it, much less an articulated adequate model'. 'The meanings which the ethnographer seeks to discover may be implicit, not explicit. They may not lie in individual items (words, objects, persons) that can be talked about, but in connections that can only gradually be discerned' (Hymes, 1996: 9; see also Blommaert & Dong, 2010: 2–3; Rampton et al., 2004: 3). It is through gradually establishing these 'connections' that I came to understand the research site. What I learned later in an individual case becomes part of a larger story.

The ethnographic interview pays attention not only to what is said, but also to how it is said, which can be crucial in getting the intended meaning and viewpoints (Blommaert & Dong, 2010: 43; Warren, 2001: 85). This then leads to the importance of making observations. As I have shown, through observing students talking with teachers on campus, observing daily lives on the local street and taking photographs, the observations in the present study served as the means to both gain a better understanding of my participants and their life before actual interviews were conducted, and supplement and refine the knowledge I learned during interviews. These are complementary ways of learning.

- Adaptability

While, as mentioned earlier, there were plans for my fieldwork, the actual fieldwork process was also contingent on the realities of the field. The plans only served as a rough guide; they kept being revised based on the actual situational affordances and constraints of the field. As I have shown in Chapter 2, the fieldwork involved a constant process of adjusting my understanding of the field itself and revising my perspectives and questions toward the various happenings. Also, unexpected questions kept coming up during the fieldwork, which were interesting enough to justify some adaptability and flexibility of my plan. As Blommaert and Dong (2010: 1) note, 'the only way forward is to adapt your plan and ways of going about things to the rules of everyday reality'; 'if these [events and processes] are complex, the analysis is complex; if they contained paradoxes, such paradoxes will also emerge in the analysis' (Blommaert & Dong, 2010: 85).

Such change in research plans and process might be seen as disturbing, especially to someone with a positivistic mindset. But this is actually what differentiates ethnographic work from many other approaches. Indeed, Hymes (1996: 7; see also Blommaert & Dong, 2010: 12; Rampton *et al.*, 2004: 2) stresses, 'it is of the essence of the method that initial questions may change during the course of inquiry. ...an essential characteristic of ethnography is that it is open-ended, subject to self-correction during the process of inquiry itself'.

- Reflexivity

As the researcher adapts his/her plans to best reproduce a 'mirror' image of the field (Blommaert & Dong, 2010: 85), it also needs to be remembered that hardly anything is an 'objective' image. This is because ethnography is 'interpretative research in a situated, real environment, based on interaction between the researcher and the subject(s), hence, fundamentally *subjective* in nature' (Blommaert & Dong, 2010: 17, italics added). My research is certainly guided by my central concern about language and social change, and therefore there might be other aspects of tourism in Yangshuo to which I was blind. Also, as the readers can tell, my own identity as a young Chinese female in many ways shapes the data collection process and methods: I was taken as an English language learner during the first few days of my fieldwork; I was not approached by disguised prostitutes even though this underground practice was not uncommon locally for male tourists; I did not go to nightclubs due to safety concerns, or my own conservativeness. There might also be other issues of which I am unaware. In other words, my own scholarly position and social identity very largely determine the type of facts I am interested in. As Hymes (1996: 13) puts it most emphatically, 'there is no way to avoid the fact that the ethnographer himself or herself is a factor in the inquiry'. But at the same time, my own status also provides perhaps unique perspectives into the social change of Yangshuo. As Rampton (2006: 392) notes, 'the researcher's own cultural and interpretive capacities are crucial in making sense of the complex intricacies of situated everyday activity among the people being studied'. In other words, I am part of the story being told here.

• Partiality

This leads to the final point I want to consider – partiality. The story here is partial not only because I am telling it from my own perspective, but also because it touches upon the often debated issues of representativeness and generalization in ethnographic research.

The tourism site of West Street, Yangshuo, as well as the claims made about it here, is not to be taken as reflecting a prototypical tourism site in China. Actually, it can be said to be a quite exceptional case of tourism development (see Chapter 1). But at the same time, this is also a most 'telling case' (Heath & Street, 2008: 64) because it speaks most directly to the research paradigm of the sociolinguistics of mobility. As Rampton (2006) observes, in ethnographic research,

> rather than taking sole responsibility for a general claim which stands or falls in subsequent argument, the objective is to build towards cumulative, comparative generalizations, sharing the responsibility for doing so with critical but cooperative readers (Hymes, 1980: 119ff.). By specifying as many of the conditioning factors as can be reasonably identified, there is an attempt to enhance the comparability and translatability of the

account, saying in effect: 'these are the practices I found, and this was the situation. Look at it in detail. How does it compare with the practices and situations you're studying? Are there processes and conditions that compare with things you've observed? Are your processes a bit different? What is it in our two situations that could account for these similarities and differences?' (Rampton, 2006: 402–403; see also Blommaert & Dong, 2010: 16–17)

Theoretical Implications

Sociolinguistics of globalization

Throughout this book, I have underscored the complex, multifaceted and unpredictable nature of globalization. Here, I provide some further discussion on the various dimensions of globalization, including the materiality of globalization, discourses on globalization, the imagination of globalization, globalization and social class and the power of globalization.

First, globalization involves social changes including linguistic, cultural, economic, social and geographical transformation that unfold through a contingent historical process. Understanding these varied processes involves tracing social change along the multiple trajectories of mobility and delineating the local process of meaning-making. In Yangshuo, we have seen that language is appropriated and justified as an important symbolic resource for constructing and branding globality; the social transformation involves geographic changes and increasing human diversity; there are also changes in business types and styles during different waves of tourism development. Also, the boundaries between domains, e.g. education, tourism and work, are sometimes blurred, illustrating what Cohen and Cohen (2012: 2181) observe as 'the late modern process of de-differentiation in social life'.

Second, globalization is also a strong discourse rooted in commercialization and consumption. I have shown that the meaning of globalization and the significance of the 'global village' are constructed through tourism promotional discourses. In these promotional discourses, the consumption of Western food and talking to international travelers in English are highlighted. In other words, linguistic and cultural diversities brought about by global mobilities are celebrated and commodified for touristic consumption, thereby producing 'discourses-on-globalization' (Blommaert, 2010: 1; see also Urry, 2000: 12). In these discursive representations, as I have shown, globalization is an embodied experience; it is concrete, celebratory and experiential, instead of being abstract or grand; diversity is to be experienced and consumed, whether it is touristic travel in the global village or talking to foreigners as part of the English educational tourism.

Third, experiences of globalization are both real and imagined, as indicated by the different ways that people conceptualize and experience globalization. While there are indeed material processes involved in the construction of the 'global village', it is also as much a discursive construct as a product of the imagination and aspiration. We see this through the performance of touristic identities by post-tourists, and through the relentless pursuit of English by language learners, both of whom embody the appeal and imperative force of globalization. At the same time, we also see critical minds who are caught in tensions and struggles, to whom the term 'global village' carries ambiguous or even pejorative meanings. Therefore, it would be futile to debate whether West Street, Yangshuo, is indeed a global village. Similar to what Anderson (1983) suggests about the imagined nature of community, the global village here is also arguably imagined, through relevant discourses of celebrated diversity, harmonious living, interracial interaction, fraternity and friendship, and also through the technologization of communication, the reduction of social complexity and the commodification of language and culture. To borrow the words of Anderson (1983: 6), global villages cannot be distinguished 'by their falsity/genuineness, but [only] by the style in which they are imagined'.

Also, the attractions of the 'global village', that is, the xiaozi lifestyle and the opportunity to practice English with foreigners, appear to correspond to a sense of being global for lower-middle-class Chinese people. These are domestic Chinese tourists with little or no overseas experience and/or knowledge of English, who aspire to a global experience. Crossing into English, drinking coffee and practicing spoken English with foreigners, these practices may not carry similar meanings for people from a different nationality, race or social class. Such a differentiated experience of globalization based on social class can also been seen in the stance that anti-tourists take on post-tourists and the global village. Anti-tourists ridicule and criticize the post-tourists as being superficial and pretentious, thereby demonstrating a sophisticated stance taken on higher moral, educational and social class grounds. The different touristic experiences and stances therefore reflect the social stratification of Chinese society wherein people from different social classes have different understandings of and stances on consumption and global experience.

Finally, as globalization provides opportunities for imagining an alternative way of life, it also excludes and marginalizes. Throughout the book, I have also shown that there are various tensions involved in this 'global village', whether it is for tourists, English learners, local foreigners or business owners. The anti-tourists' contempt for post-tourists' behavior and for the loss of local tradition; the first wave of business owners feel frustrated with the mass commercialization of West Street; local foreigners are caught up in interactional straining. The contestations and tensions are not to be interpreted defensively in the sense of people lamenting over a lost residential neighborhood, as Massey (1993) cautions against. Rather, the tensions we see in the 'global village' show the power of space, more specifically, the power of neoliberal globalization. In the case of Yangshuo, the excluding power of space arises largely from the mobilization and commodification of varied linguistic and semiotic resources, resulting in contentious ways of being, behaving and living. As nicely summarized by Appadurai (2010: 6), globalization is 'a cover term for a world of disjunctive flows – produces problems that manifest themselves in intensely local forms but have contexts that are anything but local'. It is therefore important to pay attention to the tensions, anxieties and conflicts in the study of globalization.

English as a global language

The re-evaluation, appropriation and commodification of English, as observed in Yangshuo, reproduce English as a global language; however, as I mentioned, its importance lies also in representing a 'semiotic opportunity' (Blommaert, 2010) for the local tourism economy. Indeed, the English language undergoes a process of resignification as a local practice (Pennycook, 2010). Its indexical meaning is not transparent, but is constantly constructed and promoted by tourism discourses in the media and lived out by people themselves, as shown in their xiaozi taste and style (see Chapter 3) and working professional identity (see Chapter 5). In this sense, the value of English is not absolute, but only manifested as it is constantly being promoted and lived out in people's everyday practices.

Also, even when it comes to people for whom English carries uncontested significance (e.g. post-tourists and language learners), the value of English is not absolute but constrained. In particular for the latter, the English they acquire might only operate within a particular professional sector, that is, the lower-middle-class job market in China. Their English may well lose its competitiveness as they try to compete in large-scale transnational companies, which may well have higher requirements or simply hire people with good qualifications or even overseas educational backgrounds. In this sense, the English educational tourism in Yangshuo constitutes a section of the English market in China, attracting mainly adult language learners from lower-middle-class backgrounds who find themselves under constant pressure to improve their English in the ever more competitive job market in globalizing China. Also, due to their educational backgrounds, the English they acquire in Yangshuo may carry limited transfer value in terms of achieving culture or economic capital through linguistic capital.

China and globalization

Following from the above, this study also contributes to our understanding of a globalizing China. While scholars in Chinese studies have mainly addressed the globalization of China through the macro perspective of international politics and trade, or envisioned the future of China's 'going global' policy, this study shows that a more local perspective can also help us understand the various cultural, linguistic and spatial ordering and transformations in an increasingly globalizing China. Careful attention to the local reveals the complex ways that local and trans-local factors interact, showing how local transformations only evolve contingently at the nexus of local, national and global forces, and providing insights into a changing Chinese society.

The changes in West Street, Yangshuo, during the past three decades reflect changes in Chinese society in multiple ways. When the local government needed to assume more autonomy for economic development under a market economy in the 1990s, turning to a tourism-based economy largely capitalized on an emerging domestic tourism market and the desire to enter the global order (Urry, 2002). In other words, the turn from an agriculture- to a tourism-based economy was largely driven by changing ideologies toward mobility, tourism and English within Chinese society. We see how mobility in general, and tourism mobility in particular, are linked up with discourses and practices of consumption and new ways of being and behaving in a globalizing China. The idea of mobility, as discussed in preceding chapters, represents a departure from the old politics of control to a new ideology of self-governance, performance and self-improvement, as domestic Chinese people embrace mobility and diversity in this global village. At the same time, the significance of the 'global village' in Yangshuo corresponds more to people from the emerging lower middle class, who have not quite learned to speak English, or have had no overseas experience. Such 'differentiated mobility' (Massey, 1993: 61), in other words, reflects the stratification of Chinese society wherein people from different social backgrounds perceive and experience globalization in different ways. In this sense, what is observed in Yangshuo could perhaps be best summarized as 'aspiring to be global'.

Appendix A

Transcription Conventions

((laughter))	Laughter
...	Omitted text
[italicized]	Author's translation of Chinese in interviews conducted mainly in English
[ ]	Author's comments
Italicized bold words	English words as originally used in tourist writings

Appendix B

A café with books for sale (Photo by author, 2011)

Appendix C

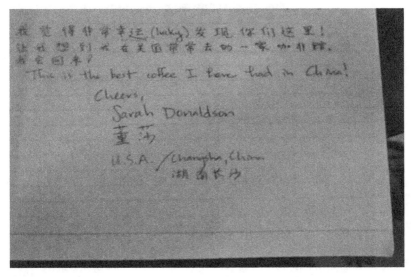

A customer's message in a coffee shop (Photo by author, 2011)

Appendix D

Stone carving of 'Yangshuo' on the bank of the Li River (Photo by author, 2011)

Appendix E

Year	2000	2001	2002	2003	2004	2005	2006	2007	2008	2009	2010
Number of tourists in total	229	240	280	282	320.2	353.5	415	516.3	559.1	720	811.3
Number of foreign tourists	38	37	39	23	38.5	63.8	82	86.6	89.9	101	123.8
Number of people stayed overnight	17.7	21	29.6	23.3	51.2	60.9	118.7	142.7	157	212.3	279.2
Average number of days stayed	1.44	1.25	1.2	1.32	1.24	1.13	1.17	1.38	1.38	1.36	1.38
Number of farmers doing tourism	0.6	0.8	1	1.3	1.45	1.5	1.8	2.5	3.5	3.8	5
Total revenue	1.85	2.14	2.41	2.44	4.06	5.51	9.64	12.77	17.9	24.2	31.5

Tourism statistics for Yangshuo: 2000–2010 (number of people: 10,000; unit of money: one hundred million Chinese yuan)

References

A cloud in the heart (2005) Xiǎozī life in Yangshuo, Guilin. See http://destguides.ctrip.com/journals-review-d702-r857673-detail.html (accessed 2 September 2010).

A Fast-Developing Tourism County: Yangshuo in the Past 20 Years of Open-Up and Reform (1999) (1978.12–1998.12) [《腾飞的中国旅游名县—阳朔县改革开放二十年 (1978.12–1998.12)》]. Yangshuo: Yangshuo County Press.

Amin, A. (2013) Land of strangers. *Identities: Global Studies in Cultural and Power* 20 (1), 1–8.

Anderson, B. (1983) *Imagined Communities: Reflections on the Origin and Spread of Nationalism.* London: Verso.

Appadurai, A. (2010) Grassroots globalization and the research imagination. *Public Culture* 12 (1), 1–19.

Arlt, W.G. (2008) Chinese tourists in 'elsewhereland': Behaviour and perceptions of mainland Chinese tourists at different destinations. In J. Cochrane (ed.) *Asian Tourism: Growth and Change* (pp. 135–144). Oxford: Elsevier.

Bai, L. (2001) Tourism and historical memory: A case study of the social movement of Manchu identity reconstruction. In C.B. Tan, S.C.H. Cheung and H. Yang (eds) *Tourism, Anthropology, and China* (pp. 237–253). Bangkok: White Lotus Press.

Bamboo (2002) *Guide for being xiǎozī at Yangshuo.* See http://www.wwfchina.org/bbs/redirect.php?tid=56269andgoto=lastpost (accessed 2 September 2010).

Bartelson, J. (2000) Three concepts of globalization. *International Sociology* 15 (2), 180–196.

Bao, X. (2002) *Xiǎozī Taste and Style* [《小资情调—一个逐渐形成的阶级及 其生活品味》]. Changchun: Jilin Photography Publishing House.

Bao, J. and Sun, J. (2007) Differences in community participation in tourism development between China and the West. *Chinese Sociology and Anthropology* 39, 9–27.

Bauman, R. (1999) Genre. *Journal of Linguistic Anthropology* 9 (1–2), 84–87.

Bauman, R. (2011) Commentary: Foundations in performance. *Journal of Sociolinguistics* 15 (5), 707–720.

Bell, A (2011) Falling in love again and again: Marlene Dietrich and the iconization of non-native English. *Journal of Sociolinguistics* 15 (5), 627–656.

Bell, A. and Gibson, A. (2011) Staging language: An introduction to the sociolinguistics of performance. *Journal of Sociolinguistics* 15 (5), 555–572.

Bian, Y. (2009) Urban occupational mobility and employment institutions: Hierarchy, market, and networks in a mixed system. In D. Davis and F. Wang (eds) *Creating*

Wealth and Poverty in Post-Socialist China (pp. 172–192). Stanford, CA: Stanford University Press.

Bigtomato (2007[2004]) *An Intoxicating West Street* [《在西街快乐中毒》]. Guilin: Guangxi People's Publishing House.

Block, D. (2002) 'McCommunication': A problem in the frame for SLA. In D. Block and D. Cameron (eds) *Globalization and Language Teaching* (pp. 117–133). London/New York: Routledge.

Blommaert, J. (2003) Commentary: A sociolinguistics of globalization. *Journal of Sociolinguistics* 7 (4), 607–623.

Blommaert, J. (2007a) On scope and depth in linguistic ethnography. *Journal of Sociolinguistics* 11 (5), 682–688.

Blommaert, J. (2007b) Sociolinguistics and discourse analysis: Orders of indexicality and polycentricity. *Journal of Multicultural Discourses* 2, 115–130.

Blommaert, J. (2010) *The Sociolinguistics of Globalization*. Cambridge/New York: Cambridge University Press.

Blommaert, J. (2012) *Ethnography, Superdiversity and Linguistic Landscapes: Chronicles of Complexity*. Bristol: Multilingual Matters.

Blommaert, J. and Dong, J. (2010) *Ethnographic Fieldwork: A Beginner's Guide*. Bristol: Multilingual Matters.

Blommaert, J. and Rampton, B. (2011) Language and superdiversity: A position chapter. *Working Papers in Urban Language and Literacies*. Paper 70.

Blommaert, J., Collins, J. and Slembrouck, S. (2005) Polycentricity and interactional regimes in 'global neighborhoods'. *Ethnography* 6 (2), 205–235.

Bodomo, A. (2010) Documentation and revitalization of the Zhuang language and culture of Southwestern China through linguistic fieldwork. *Diaspora, Indigenous, and Minority Education: Studies of Migration, Integration, Equity, and Cultural Survival* 4 (3), 179–191.

Bolton, K. (2003) *Chinese Englishes: A Sociolinguistic History*. Cambridge: Cambridge University Press.

Bolton, K. and Graddol, D. (2012) English in China today. *English Today* 28, 3–9.

Brenner, N. and Theodore, N. (2002) Cities and the geographies of 'actually existing neoliberalism'. *Antipode* 34 (3), 349–379.

Brother Big Horse (2006) Travelling fugue at West Street: Suggestions and strategies. See http://blog.sina.com.cn/s/blog_59407ea90100095y.html (accessed 2 September 2010).

Bruner, E.M. (1986) Ethnography as narrative. In V.W. Turner and E.M. Bruner (eds) *The Anthropology of Experience* (pp. 139–158). Urbana, IL: University of Illinois Press.

Bruner, E.M. (1991) Transformation of self in tourism. *Annals of Tourism Research* 18 (2), 238–250.

Bucholtz, M. (2003) Sociolinguistic nostalgia and the authentication of identity. *Journal of Sociolinguistics* 7 (3), 398–416.

Bucholtz, M. and Hall, K. (2005) Identity and interaction: A sociocultural linguistic approach. *Discourse Studies* 7 (4–5), 585–614.

Chen, J. (2009) The soft power of culture in Yangshuo tourism development. In T. Tang and C. Xianzhong (eds) *Scientific Development of Guangxi Tourism: Exploring the Yangshuo Phenomenon* [《广西旅游与科学发展—阳朔现象探究》] (pp. 171–175). Beijing: Huaxia Publishing House.

Chen, W. (2009) Opening our mind for development: Thoughts on the economic development of Yangshuo. In T. Tang and C. Xianzhong (eds) *Scientific Development* of Guangxi Tourism: Exploring the Yangshuo Phenomenon (pp. 357–362). Beijing: Huaxia Publishing House.

Chen, X. (2009) Promoting Yangshuo: Towards a scientific development of the county's economy. In T. Tang and C. Xianzhong (eds) Scientific Development of Guangxi Tourism: Exploring the Yangshuo Phenomenon (pp. 74–84). Beijing: Huaxia Publishing House.

Chen, X. (2016) Linguascaping the Other: Travelogues' representations of Chinese languages. Multilingua 35 (5), 513–534.

Cheng, T. and Selden, M. (1994) The origins and social consequences of China's Hukou system. The China Quarterly 139, 644–668.

Cho, J. (2012) Global fatigue: Transnational markets, linguistic capital, and Korean-American male English teachers in South Korea. Journal of Sociolinguistics 16 (2), 218–237.

Cohen, E. (1984) The sociology of tourism: Approaches, issues, and findings. Annual Review of Sociology 10, 373–392.

Cohen, E. and Cohen, S.A. (2012) Current sociological theories and issues in tourism. Annals of Tourism Research 39 (4), 2177–2202.

Contemporary China: Guangxi [《当代中国的广西》] (2009) Beijing: Contemporary China Publishing House.

Cooper, C. and Latham, J. (1988) English educational tourism. Tourism Management 331–334.

Coupland, N. (2003) Introduction: Sociolinguistics and globalization. Journal of Sociolinguistics 7 (4), 465–472.

Coupland, N. (2010a) Introduction: Sociolinguistics in the global era. In N. Coupland (ed.) The Handbook of Language and Globalization (pp. 1–27). Malden, MA: Wiley-Blackwell.

Coupland, N. (ed.) (2010b) The Handbook of Language and Globalization. Malden, MA: Wiley-Blackwell.

Coupland, N., Garrett, P. and Bishop, H. (2005) Wales underground: Discursive frames and authenticities in Welsh mining heritage tourism events. In A. Jaworski and A. Pritchard (eds) Discourse, Communication and Tourism (pp. 199–222). Clevedon: Channel View Publications.

Cresswell, T. (2009) Place. See http://booksite.elsevier.com/brochures/hugy/SampleContent/Place.pdf (accessed 20 November 2013).

Croll, E. (2006) China's New Consumers: Social Development and Domestic Demand. New York: Routledge.

Dann, G. (1996) The Language of Tourism: A Sociolinguistic Perspective. Wallingford: CABI.

Dann, G. and Cohen, E. (1991) Sociology of tourism. Annals of Tourism Research 18, 155–169.

Eckert, P. (2003) Sociolinguistics and authenticity: An elephant in the room. Journal of Sociolinguistics 7 (3), 392–431.

Edmondson, J.A. (1994) Change and variation in Zhuang. In K. Adams and T. Hudak (eds) Papers from the Second Annual Meeting of the Southeast Asian Linguistics Society (pp. 147–185). Tempe, AZ: Arizona State University Program for Southeast Asian Studies.

Erickson, F. (1986) Qualitative methods in research on teaching. In M.C. Wittrock (ed.) Handbook of Research on Teaching (3rd edn; pp. 119–161). New York: Macmillan.

Farrer, J. (2014) Foreigner Street: Urban citizenship in multicultural Shanghai. In N. Kim (ed.) *Multicultural Challenges and Redefining Identity in East Asia* (pp. 17–44). London: Ashgate.

Foucault, M. (1988) Technologies of the self. In L.H. Martin, H. Gutman and P.H. Hutton (eds) *Technologies of the Self: A Seminar with Michel Foucault* (pp. 16–49). Amherst, MA: University of Massachusetts Press.

Foucault, M. (1991) Governmentality. In G. Burchell, C. Gordon and P. Miller (eds) *The Foucault Effect: Studies in Governmentality* (pp. 87–104). Hemel Hempstead: Harvester Wheatsheaf.

Gao, S. and Park, J.S.-Y. (2015) Space and language learning under the neoliberal economy. *L2 Journal* 7, 78–96.

Gao, S., Huang, S. and Huang, Y. (2009) Rural tourism development in China. *International Journal of Tourism Research* 11, 439–450.

Gao, X. (2009) The 'English Corner' as an out-of-class learning activity. *ELT Journal* 63, 60–67.

Gao, X. (2012) The study of English in China as a patriotic enterprise. *World Englishes* 31 (3), 351–365.

Garrett, P. (2010) Meanings of 'globalization': East and West. In N. Coupland (ed.) *The Handbook of Language and Globalization* (pp. 447–474). Malden, MA: Wiley-Blackwell.

Gaudio, R.P. (2003) Coffeetalk: Starbucks™ and the commercialization of casual conversation. *Language in Society* 32, 659–691.

George, S. (1999) *A Short History of Neoliberalism*. New York: Global Policy Forum. See http://www.globalpolicy.org/globaliz/econ/histneol.htm.

Gershon, I. (2011) 'Neoliberal Agency'. *Current Anthropology* 52, 537–555.

Giddens, A. (2000) *Runaway World: How Globalization is Reshaping Our Lives*. New York: Routledge.

Gieryn, T.F. (2000) A space for place in sociology. *Annual Review of Sociology* 26, 463–496.

Goffman, E. (1959) *The Presentation of Self in Everyday Life*. London: Penguin Books.

Goffman, E. (1963) *Behavior in Public Places: Notes on the Social Organization of Gatherings*. New York: The Free Press.

Gotham, K.F. (2005) Tourism gentrification: The case of New Orleans' Vieux Carre (French Quarter). *Urban Studies* 42 (7), 1099–1121.

Graburn, N.H.H. (2002) The ethnographic tourist. In G. Dann (ed.) *The Tourist as a Metaphor of the Social World* (pp. 19–39). New York: CABI Publishing.

Gray, J. (2010) The branding of English and the culture of the new capitalism: Representations of the world of work in English language textbooks. *Applied Linguistics* 31, 714–733.

Gumperz, J., Jupp, T. and Roberts, C. (1981) *Crosstalk: A Study of Cross-cultural Communication: Background Material and Notes to Accompany the BBC film*. Southall: National Centre for Industrial Language Training.

Guo, W. (1999) Making new breakthroughs in the new century. In *A Fast-Developing Tourism County: Yangshuo in the Past 20 Years of Open-Up and Reform* [《腾飞的"中国旅游名县"—阳朔县改革开放二十年》] (pp. 18–23). Yangshuo: Yangshuo County Publishing House.

Hannam, K., Sheller, M. and Urry, J. (2006) Editorial: Mobilities, immobilities and moorings. *Mobilities* 1, 1–22.

Harvey, D. (1993) From space to place and back again. In J. Bird, B. Curtis, T. Putnam and L. Tickner (eds) *Mapping the Futures: Local Cultures, Global Change* (pp. 3–29). London/New York: Routledge.

Harvey, D. (2005) *A Brief History of Neoliberalism*. Oxford/New York: Oxford University Press.

He, Z. (2011) 'Travel abroad' to West Street, Yangshuo. *Contemporary Guangxi* [《当代广西》] 174, 56–57.

Heath, S.B. and Street, B.V. (2008) *On Ethnography: Approaches to Language and Literacy Research*. New York: Teachers College Press.

Heller, M. (2003) Globalization, the new economy, and the commodification of language and identity. *Journal of Sociolinguistics* 7 (4), 473–492.

Heller, M. (2010) Language as resource in the globalized new economy. In N. Coupland (ed.) *The Handbook of Language and Globalization* (pp. 349–365). Malden, MA: Wiley-Blackwell.

Heller, M. (2017) Can language be a commodity? In J.R. Cavanaugh and S. Shankar (eds) *Language and Materiality: Ethnographic and Theoretical Explorations* (pp. 252–254). Cambridge: Cambridge University Press.

Henry, E.S. (2010) Interpretations of 'Chinglish': Native speakers, language learners and the enregisterment of a stigmatized code. *Language in Society* 39 (5), 669–688.

Hoffman, L. (2010) *Patriotic Professionalism in Urban China: Fostering Talent*. Philadelphia, PA: Temple University Press.

Holborow, M. (2015) *Language and Neoliberalism*. Abingdon: Routledge.

Hu, G. (2005) English language education in China: Policies, progress and problems. *Language Policy* 4, 5–24.

Hu, G. and McKay, S.L. (2012) English language education in East Asia: Some recent developments. *Journal of Multilingual and Multicultural Development* 33 (4), 345–362.

Huang, Q. (2009) New strategies of scientific development: Implications of the 'Yangshuo phenomenon'. In T. Tang and C. Xianzhong (eds) *Scientific Development of Guangxi Tourism: Exploring the Yangshuo Phenomenon* (pp. 17–22). Beijing: Huaxia Publishing House.

Hymes, D. (1977) The scope of sociolinguistics. In D. Hymes (ed.) *Foundations in Sociolinguistics: An Ethnographic Approach* (pp. 193–210). London: Tavistock.

Hymes, D. (1996) What is ethnography? In D. Hymes (ed.) *Ethnography, Linguistics, Narrative Inequality: Toward an Understanding of Voice* (pp. 3–16). London/Bristol, PA: Taylor & Francis.

Irvine, J. (1989) When talk isn't cheap: Language and political economy. *American Ethnologist* 16 (2), 248–267.

Irvine, J. and Gal, S. (2000) Language ideology and linguistic differentiation. In H.V. Kroskrity (ed.) *Regimes of Language: Ideologies, Polities, and Identities* (pp. 35–84). Santa Fe, NM/Oxford: School of American Research Press.

Jacquemet, M. (2005) Transidiomatic practices: Language and power in the age of globalization. *Language & Communication* 25 (3), 257–277.

Jaffe, A. (2009) Introduction: The sociolinguistics of stance. In A.M. Jaffe (ed.) *Stance: Sociolinguistic Perspectives* (pp. 1–28). Oxford/New York: Oxford University Press.

Jamal, T. and Hill, S. (2002) The home and the world: (Post)touristic spaces of (in)authenticity? In G. Dann (ed.) *The Tourist as a Metaphor of the Social World* (pp. 77–108). Wallingford: CABI.

Jaworski, A. and Thurlow, C. (2009) Taking an elitist stance: Ideology and the discursive production of social distinction. In A.M. Jaffe (ed.) *Stance: Sociolinguistic Perspectives* (pp. 195–226). Oxford/New York: Oxford University Press.

Jaworski, A. and Thurlow, C. (2010) Language and the globalizing habitus of tourism: Toward a sociolinguistics of fleeting relationships. In N. Coupland (ed.) *The Handbook of Language and Globalization* (pp. 255–286). Malden, MA: Wiley-Blackwell.

Ji, F. (2004) Linguistic engineering in Mao's China: The case of English language teaching. *New Zealand Journal of Asian Studies* 6, 83–99.

Jiang, Y. (2009) Showing the humanistic and natural wonders: Thoughts on the 'Yangshuo phenomenon' and the city development of Guilin. In T. Tang and C. Xianzhong (eds) *Scientific Development of Guangxi Tourism: Exploring the Yangshuo Phenomenon* (pp. 198–203). Beijing: Huaxia Publishing House.

Jin, L. and Cortazzi, M. (2002) English language teaching in China: A bridge to the future. *Asia Pacific Journal of Education* 22 (2), 53–64.

Johnstone, B. (2004) Place, globalization, and linguistic variation. In C. Fought (ed.) *Sociolinguistic Variation: Critical Reflections* (pp. 65–83). New York/Oxford: Oxford University Press.

Johnstone, B. (2010) Language and geographical space. In P. Auer and J.E. Schmidt (eds) *Language and Space: An International Handbook of Linguistic Variation* (pp. 1–17). Berlin: Walter de Gruyter.

Kearney, M. (1995) The local and the global: The anthropology of globalization and transnationalism. *Annual Review of Anthropology* 24, 547–565.

Kelly-Holmes, H. and Pietikainen, S. (2014) Commodifying Sami culture in an indigenous tourism site. *Journal of Sociolinguistics* 18, 518–538.

Kobayashi, Y. (2011) Expanding-circle students learning 'standard English' in the outer-circle Asia. *Journal of Multilingual and Multicultural Development* 32 (3), 235–248.

Kramsch, C. (2005) Post 9/11: Foreign languages between knowledge and power. *Applied Linguistics* 26 (4), 545–567.

Krashen, S. (2006) Letter: English villages and hype. *Taipei Times*, 20 April. See http://www.taipeitimes.com/News/editorials/archives/2006/04/20/2003303683 (accessed 28 June 2013).

Kubota, R. (2011) Questioning linguistic instrumentalism: English, neoliberalism, and language tests in Japan. *Linguistics and Education* 22 (3), 248–260.

Leach, M. (2004) Yangshuo changes from 1984. See http://community.travelchinaguide.com/review2.asp?i=113 (accessed 8 November 2010).

Leiper, N. (1990) *Tourism Systems: An Interdisciplinary Perspective*. Palmerston North: Massey University.

Leite, N. and Graburn, N. (2009) Anthropological interventions in tourism studies. In T. Jamal and M. Robinson (eds) *The SAGE Handbook of Tourism Studies* (pp. 35–64). Los Angeles, CA/London: SAGE.

Levinson, S. (1979) Activity types and language. *Linguistics* 17, 365–399.

Liu, F. (2005) Laowai as spokesperson for Yangshuo. See http://www.people.com.cn/GB/news/37146/45769/3643775.html (accessed 20 March 2011).

Lonely Planet China (1988) Hawthorn: Lonely Planet Publications.

Lonely Planet China (1994) Hawthorn: Lonely Planet Publications.

Lonely Planet China (1998) Hawthorn: Lonely Planet Publications.

MacCannell, D. (1989) Introduction. *Annals of Tourism Research* 16, 1–6.

Massey, D. (1993) Power-geometry and a progressive sense of place. In J. Bird, B. Curtis, T. Putnam and L. Tickner (eds) *Mapping the Futures: Local Cultures, Global Change* (pp. 60–70). London/New York: Routledge.

Massey, D. (1994) A global sense of place. In D. Massey (ed.) *Space, Place, and Gender* (pp. 146–156). Minneapolis, MN: University of Minnesota Press.

Mavrič, M. and Urry, J. (2009) Tourism studies and the new mobilities paradigm. In T. Jamal and M. Robinson (eds) *The SAGE Handbook of Tourism Studies* (pp. 645–657). Los Angeles, CA/London: SAGE.

McCabe, S. (2005) 'Who is a tourist'?: A critical review. *Tourist Studies* 5, 85–106.

Nanning Evening Paper (2013) Zhuang-Chinese sign boards to be used in public places in Nanning. See http://www.nnnews.net/news/201306/t20130619_549000.html (accessed 9 September 2013).

Nash, D. (1981) Tourism as an anthropological subject. *Current Anthropology* 22 (5), 461–468.

Nash, D. and Smith, V. (1991) Anthropology and tourism. *Annals of Tourism Research* 18, 12–25.

nowherekid (2010) West Street, Yangshuo: Lose and indulgence. See http://travel.sina.com.cn/china/2010-03-18/1042130989.shtml (accessed 2 September 2010).

Nyíri, P. (2009) Between encouragement and control: Tourism, modernity and discipline in China. In T. Winter, P. Teo and T.C. Chang (eds) *Asia on Tour* (pp. 153–169). New York: Routledge.

Nyíri, P. (2010) *Mobility and Cultural Authority in Contemporary China*. Seattle, WA: University of Washington Press.

Olssen, M. (2006) Understanding the mechanisms of neoliberal control: Lifelong learning, flexibility and knowledge capitalism. *International Journal of Lifelong Education* 25 (3) 213–230.

Ong, A. (2006) *Neoliberalism as Exception: Mutations in Citizenship and Sovereignty*. Durham NC: Duke University Press.

Ong, A. (2007) Neoliberalism as a mobile technology. *Transactions of the Institute of British Geographers* 32 (1), 3–8.

Ong, A. (2008) Self-fashioning Shanghainese: Dancing across spheres of value. In L. Zhang and A. Ong (eds) *Privatizing China: Socialism from Afar* (pp. 182–196). Ithaca, NY: Cornell University Press.

Pan, L. and Block, D. (2011) English as a 'global language' in China: An investigation into learners' and teachers' language beliefs. *System* 39 (3), 391–402.

Pan, Q. (2005) A study of the impact of tourism development on language cultural landscape: A case study of Xi'an. *Tourism Tribune* 20, 19–25.

Pang, J., Zhou, X. and Fu, Z. (2002) English for international trade: China enters the WTO. *World Englishes* 21 (2), 201–216.

Park, J.S-Y. (2009) *The Local Construction of a Global Language: Ideologies of English in South Korea*. Berlin/Boston, MA: De Gruyter Mouton.

Park, J.S-Y. (2010a) Naturalization of competence and the neoliberal subject: Success stories of English language learning in the Korean conservative press. *Journal of Linguistic Anthropology* 20 (1), 22–38.

Park, J.S-Y. (2010b) Images of 'good English' in the Korean conservative press: Three processes of interdiscursivity. *Pragmatics and Society* 1, 189–208.

Park, J.S-Y. (2011) The promise of English: Linguistic capital and the neoliberal worker in the South Korean job market. *International Journal of Bilingual Education and Bilingualism* 14 (4), 443–455.

Park, J.S.-Y. (2013) English, class and neoliberalism in South Korea. In L. Wee, R.B.H. Goh and L. Lim (eds) *The Politics of English: South Asia, Southeast Asia and the Asia Pacific* (pp. 287–302). Amsterdam/Philadelphia, PA: John Benjamins.

Park, J.S-Y. and Bae, S.H. (2009) Language ideologies in educational migration: Korean jogi yuhak families in Singapore. *Linguistics and Education* 20 (4), 366–377.

Parlow (2001) Parlow China Trip, Yangshuo/Guilin. See http://www.mytripjournal. com/travel-429-guilin-rice-paddies-rain-yangshuo-china-boat-cafe-peaks (accessed 8 November 2010).

Peck, J. and Tickell, A. (2002) Neoliberalizing space. *Antipode* 34 (3), 380–404.

Pennycook, A. (1994) *The Cultural Politics of English as an International Language.* London/New York: Longman.

Pennycook, A. (2010) *Language as a Local Practice.* Abingdon/New York: Routledge.

People's Daily (2001) More Chinese value communication skills. See http://english.peopl e.com.cn/english/200110/30/eng20011030_83476.html (accessed 16 July 2012).

Peréz-Milans, M. (2013) *Urban Schools and English Language Education in Late Modern China: A Critical Sociolinguistic Ethnography.* New York/London: Routledge.

Philips, S. (2004) Language and social inequality. In A. Duranti (ed.) *A Companion to Linguistic Anthropology* (pp. 474–495). Malden, MA: Blackwell.

Piller, I. and Cho, J. (2013) Neoliberalism as language policy. *Language in Society* 42 (1), 23–44.

Pratt, M.L. (1987) Linguistic utopias. In N. Fabb, D. Attridge, A. Durant and C. MacCabe (eds) *The Linguistics of Writing: Arguments between Language and Literature* (pp. 48–66). Manchester: Manchester University Press.

Price, G. (2014) English for all?: Neoliberalism, globalization, and language policy in Taiwan. *Language in Society* 43 (5), 567–589.

Pride, J.B. and Liu, R. (1988) Some aspects of the spread of English in China since 1949. *International Journal of Sociology of Language* 74, 41–70.

Pujolar, J. (2007) Bilingualism and the nation-state in the post-national era. In M. Heller (ed.) *Bilingualism: A Social Approach* (pp. 71–110). Basingstoke/New York: Palgrave Macmillan.

Qin, Z. (2004) The 'Yangshuo' lithoglyph. In Q. Zhen (ed.) *West Street Stories* [《西街故事》] (pp. 326–330). Nanning: Guangxi People's Publisher.

Rampton, B. (1995) *Crossing: Language and Ethnicity Among Adolescents.* London/New York: Longman.

Rampton, B. (1997a) Retuning in applied linguistics. *International Journal of Applied Linguistics* 7 (1), 3–25.

Rampton, B. (1997b) A sociolinguistic perspective on L2 communication strategies. In G. Kasper and E. Kellerman (eds) *Communication Strategies: Psycholinguistic and Sociolinguistic Perspectives* (pp. 272–303). London: Longman.

Rampton, B. (1997c) Second language research in late modernity: A response to Firth and Wagner. *The Modern Language Journal* 81 (3), 329–333.

Rampton, B. (2000) Speech community. *Working Papers in Urban Language and Literacies.* Paper 15.

Rampton, B. (2006) *Language in Late Modernity: Interaction in an Urban School.* Cambridge/New York: Cambridge University Press.

Rampton, B. (2009) Speech community and beyond. In N. Coupland and A. Jaworski (eds) *The New Sociolinguistics Reader* (pp. 694–713). Basingstoke/New York: Palgrave Macmillan.

Rampton, B. (2010) Speech community. In J. Jaspers, J-O. Ostman and J. Verschueren (eds) *Society and Language Use* (pp. 274–303). Amsterdam: John Benjamins.

Rampton, B. (2013) 'Agents' or 'participation'?: Sociolinguistic frameworks for the study of media engagement. *Working Papers in Urban Language & Literacies.* Paper 117.

Rampton, B., Tusting, K., Maybin, J., Barwell, R., Creese, A. and Lytra V. (2004) UK linguistic ethnography: A discussion paper. Linguistic Ethnography Forum.

Read, J. (2009) A genealogy of homo-economicus: Neoliberalism and the production of subjectivity. *Foucault Studies* 6, 25–36.

Rofel, L. (2007) *Desiring China: Experiments in Neoliberalism, Sexuality, and Public Culture*. Durham, NC/London: Duke University Press.

Sassen, S. (2002) Locating cities on global circuits. In S. Sassen (ed.) *Global Networks, Linked Cities* (pp. 1–36). London: Routledge.

Seargeant, P. (2005) 'More English than England itself': The simulation of authenticity in foreign language practice in Japan. *International Journal of Applied Linguistics* 15 (3), 326–345.

Sharma, B.K. and Phyak, P. (2017) Neoliberalism, linguistic commodification, and ethnolinguistic identity in multilingual Nepal. *Language in Society* 46 (2), 231–256.

Sheller, M. and Urry, J. (2006) The new mobilities paradigm. *Environment and Planning A* 38, 207–226.

Simpson, T. (2008) The commercialization of Macau's cafés. *Ethnography* 9, 197–234.

Stronza, A. (2001) Anthropology of tourism: Forging new ground for ecotourism and other alternatives. *Annual Review of Anthropology* 30, 261–283.

Stroud, C. and Mpendukana, S. (2009) Towards a material ethnography of linguistic landscape: Multilingualism, mobility and space in a South African township. *Journal of Sociolinguistics* 13 (3), 363–386.

Stroud, C. and Jegels, D. (2013) Semiotic landscapes and mobile narrations of place: Performing the local. *Tilburg Papers in Culture Studies*, Paper 50.

Su, X. and Teo, P. (2009) *The Politics of Heritage Tourism in China: A View from Lijiang*. London/New York: Routledge.

Tan, Z. (1999) Some thoughts on accelerating the tertiary economy of Yangshuo. In *A Fast-Developing Tourism County: Yangshuo in the Past 20 Years of Open-Up and Reform* (pp. 31–34). Yangshuo: Yangshuo County Publishing House.

The Tourism Industry in Contemporary China [《当代中国的旅游业》] (2009) Beijing: Contemporary China Publishing House.

Thurlow, C. and Jaworski, A. (2010) *Tourism Discourse: Language and Global Mobility*. Basingstoke/New York: Palgrave Macmillan.

Trottier, M. (2008) Towards a sociocultural perspective on Korean English villages: A reply to Stephen Krashen. *International Journal of Pedagogies and Learning* 4 (1), 71–91.

Tuan, Y-F. (1991) Language and the making of place: A narrative-descriptive approach. *Annals of the Association of American Geographers* 81 (4), 684–696.

Urciuoli, B. (2008) Skills and selves in the new workplace. *American Ethnologist* 35 (2), 211–228.

Uriely, N. and Reichel, A. (2000) Working tourists and their attitudes to hosts. *Annals of Tourism Research* 27 (2), 267–283.

Urry, J. (1990) The consumption of tourism. *Sociology* 24, 23–35.

Urry, J. (2000) *Sociology beyond Societies: Mobilities for the Twenty-First Century*. London/New York: Routledge.

Urry, J. (2002) *The Tourist Gaze*. London/Thousand Oaks, CA: SAGE.

Valentine, G. (2008) Living with difference: Reflections on geographies of encounter. *Progress in Human Geography* 32 (3), 323–337.

Wah, C.Y. (2009) Disorganized tourism space: Chinese tourists in an age of Asia tourism. In T. Winter, P. Teo and T.C. Chang (eds) *Asia on Tour* (pp. 67–78). New York: Routledge.

Wang, L. (2004) When English becomes big business. In T. Weiss and K. Tam (eds) *English and Globalization: Perspectives from Hong Kong and Mainland China* (pp. 149–168). Hong Kong: Chinese University Press.

Wang, N. (2000) *Tourism and Modernity: Sociological Analysis*. Amsterdam/New York: Pergamon.

Wang, J. (2005) Bourgois Bohemians in China? Neo-tribes and the urban imaginary. *The China Quarterly* 183, 532–548.

Wang, Q. (2006a) West Street: Historical stories [西街史话]. In Q. Wang (ed.) *The Wonderland of Yangshuo* [《仙境阳朔, 梦幻家园》] (pp. 108–151). Guilin: Lijiang Publishing House.

Wang, Q. (2006b) The golden sign board on West Street [西街上的金字招牌]. In Q. Wang (ed.) *The Wonderland of Yangshuo* [《仙境阳朔, 梦幻家园》] (pp. 589–590). Guilin: Lijiang Publishing House.

Wang, X. (2015) Inauthentic authenticity: Semiotic design and globalization in the margins of China. *Semiotica* 203, 227–248.

Warren, C. (2001) Qualitative interviewing. In J.F. Gubrium and J.A. Holstein (eds) *Handbook of Interview Research* (pp. 83–103). Thousand Oakes, CA: SAGE.

Wee, L. (2008) The technologization of discourse and authenticity in English language teaching. *International Journal of Applied Linguistics* 18 (3), 256–273.

West Street (2001) Yangshuo: Heaven for xiǎozī. See http://www.china.com.cn/chinese/TRsummer/75324.htm (accessed 20 September 2010).

Williams, R. (1979) *Politics and Letters*. London: New Left Books.

Winter, T. (2009) Asian tourism and the retreat of Anglo-western centrism in tourism theory. *Current Issues in Tourism* 12 (1), 21–31.

Woolard, K. (1992) Language ideology: Issues and approaches. *Pragmatics* 2 (3), 235–249.

Xiao, H. (2006) The discourse of power: Deng Xiaoping and tourism development in China. *Tourism Management* 27, 803–814.

Yan, H. (2003) Neoliberal governmentality and neohumanism: Organizing suzhi/value flow through labor recruitment networks. *Cultural Anthropology* 18 (4), 493–523.

Yan, Z. (2010) Language use in waiqi in Shanghai. See http://sspress.cass.cn/news/12914.htm (accessed 3 September 2014).

Yangshuo County Chronicles: 1986–2003 [《阳朔县志:1986–2003》] (2003) Beijing: Fangzhi Publishing House.

Yangshuo Tourism Bureau (2009) Educational Tourism. See http://www.yangshuotour.com/yangshuolvyou/xiuxueyou/2009/1226/620.html (accessed 8 November 2010).

You, T. (2013) Speaking English in wàiqī: A Chinese national characteristic. Guanchazhe. See http://www.guancha.cn/YouTianLong/2013_06_07_149717.shtml (accessed 2 September 2014).

Yu, J. (2005) Mama Moon at Yangshuo. See http://news.xinhuanet.com/video/2005-07/21/content_3247860.htm (accessed 20 March 2011).

Zhang, G. (2003) China's tourism since 1978: Policies, experiences, and lessons learned. In A. Lew, L. Yu, J. Ap and G. Zhang (eds) *Tourism in China* (pp. 13–34). New York: Haworth Hospitality Press.

Zhao, M. (1999) Thoughts on the economic development of Yangshuo. In *A Fast-Developing Tourism County: Yangshuo in the Past 20 Years of Open-Up and Reform* (pp. 42–47). Yangshuo: Yangshuo County Publishing House.

Zhao, Y. and Campbell, K.P. (1995) English in China. *World Englishes* 14 (3), 377–390.

Zheng, Y. (2014) *Contemporary China: A History since 1978*. Malden, MA: Wiley-Blackwell.

Zhou, M. (2003) *Multilingualism in China: The Politics of Writing Reforms for Minority Languages 1949–2002*. Berlin/New York: Mouton de Gruyter.

Index

CPSIA information can be obtained
at www.ICGtesting.com
Printed in the USA
JSHW031211120522
25839JS00006B/36